MW00928840

1 GOAL FOR 100 DAYS

A Motivational Journal by Kelli France

Copyright © 2023 Kelli France

Testimonials used with permission.

All Rights Reserved.

www.kellifrance.com

To my children, Savannah, Anthony, Abe, & Max.

I wrote my first book.

Now it's your turn. (wink wink)

INTRODUCTION

As I write this paragraph, I am sitting on the edge of a hotel bed, wearing a stiff hotel bathrobe and waiting for my turn to shower. It's almost midnight. My skin is red with sunburn, my body carries sand in every crack and crevice. My hair is levitating with frizz. By no means am I complaining. I had a magical day in the sun with my friends.

Still, it's an odd time and place to begin writing a book.

The old me would have let my exhaustion and the inconvenient location be the perfect excuse NOT to start this Big Scary Goal.

"I'll start tomorrow," I would say to myself as I switched off the lights. "Besides, you don't even have your laptop!" I'd reason, entirely justified.

But that's the old me.

The new me made a commitment to complete ONE goal in 100 days. Why here, on vacation? Why now, perched on the end of a strange bed? Because there are 100 days left in the year and hundreds of women have accepted the challenge to join me on this journey, starting today. I couldn't let them (or myself!) down on Day 1.

So I opened my phone and began to write.

HOW IT ALL STARTED

During the pandemic, I attended a virtual conference hosted by the company that I partner with. The keynote speaker was Michelle Poller, author of *Hello, Fears*. I was wary of how a virtual gathering would compare to our in-person conferences of the past, but Michelle infused it with energy. She was vibrant, goofy, and a whole lot of fun. And she shared my affinity for wearing bold, colorful clothing. I can still remember the bright red lipstick she wore as she spoke. She recounted a personal project where she faced 100 different fears in 100 days. I loved this idea; I am a huge fan of tackling fears. Heck, I even named my popular podcast, "Finally Fearless"!

But what I loved even more was that she did it in 100 days.

After the conference, I began texting back and forth with two friends about the presentation. We were all struck with the idea of focusing on something for 100 days.

How powerful would it be if each of us chose one simple goal and worked on it every day for 100 days? Having read the bestselling book *The One Thing* by Gary Keller and Jay Papasan, I understood the power of singular focus.

My friends and I set our goals. I'd been experiencing some health issues, so I decided mine would be to eat sugar-free and gluten-free for 100 days, to see if it helped me feel better. My friend Polly wanted to start eating dinner together with her family for 100 days. McKenzie committed to doing her 5 IPAs (income-producing activities) each day for 100 days.

McKenzie's goal got me thinking, *"What if I encouraged my team of 20,000 women to take on Mckenzie's idea: 5 IPAs each day for 100 days?"*

So I challenged my team to do just that. Then I got to thinking further—"What if I challenged my social media following to join us with their own goals?"

Thousands of people committed to the *challenge* and that's when the movement began. I called it: *1 Goal for 100 Days.*

The best part came when people began to see some wins. It was hugely fulfilling to see women from all over the world posting about their daily goals. They were gaining traction and momentum from their consistency. They were feeling more confident from showing up for themselves.

That is what this book is all about: transforming yourself from the person who WANTS to achieve goals into the person who actually DOES achieve their goals, regardless of sunburns and sand and the fact that it's almost midnight and you're supposed to be on vacation, for heaven's sake.

This book is about action, not excuses. And it's formatted to support you every day of your 100 day journey. You'll start by selecting a goal (I've made a list of 100 ideas, in case you're not yet sure what you want to do). Then print out my free tracker to mark your progress.

I walk you through the **5 C's of Success:**

1. Commit
2. Calendar
3. Cheerleader
4. Consistency
5. Cutoff

And give you my **Strategies for Starting:**

1. Start Small
2. Start Slow
3. Start Sloppy
4. Set Yourself Up for Success
5. Set Yourself Up for Setbacks

Sprinkled throughout are powerhouse quotes and inspiring testimonials from women just like you, who have taken on and successfully completed challenges ranging from 100 days of making the bed to 100 days of going to the gym!

Every day includes a blank journal page. Use the prompts provided or freewrite how you're feeling about the challenge that day.

If you picked up this journal, it's likely that you are the kind of person who a *lot of* different goals. You're my kind of person! But this book and this movement is about choosing just ONE GOAL to focus on and staying committed to it consistently for 100 days. Trust me, what you learn in the process will help you become your best self and achieve your abundant dreams.

Remember my messy Day 1 at the edge of the hotel bed? Well, 100 days later, I finished the book you hold in your hands. I can't wait to see the amazing things *you'll* accomplish in the next 100 days! Let's do this!

1 GOAL FOR 100 DAYS TRACKER

Scan the QR code below to download my free 100-Day Tracker to help you stay accountable.

100 DAILY GOAL IDEAS

Looking for ideas? Here is a list of things some of the hundreds of women in our community did for 100 days:

- 5000 steps
- 20 minute workout
- 10 minutes journaling
- 15 minute meditation
- Reach out to one person in a social network business group
- Drink half your weight in ounces of water
- Post a picture of something you're grateful for
- Walk outside
- Wake up at 6am
- 5 minutes of yoga
- Write one page of your book
- Write one paragraph of your book
- Write one sentence of your book
- No alcohol
- No soda
- No chocolate
- Read 10 minutes
- Recite an affirmation
- Follow a specific morning routine
- Read one picture book to your child
- Practice 10 minutes of a language on the Duolingo app
- Take the dog for a walk
- Draw in a sketchbook
- Paint an abstract picture

- 20 squats
- Study for the GMAT
- Write down one thing you're grateful for
- Write down one thing you're proud of yourself for
- Ride your bike
- Run for 10 minutes
- 10 push-ups each day
- Take a multivitamin
- Declutter 1 item from your wardrobe
- Declutter 1 item from your house
- Follow up with 1 person
- Wash your face
- Track your calories
- Learn 1 new person's name
- Listen to 10 minutes of a motivational podcast
- Spend 15 minutes daily planning and creating your own podcast
- Spend 15 minutes practicing a musical instrument
- Write a thank you note to someone in your life (big or small)
- Do 10 jumping jacks
- Do 30 jumping jacks
- Look up and practice a new recipe
- Keep a dream journal
- Learn the definition of one new word
- Read one poem
- Work toward memorizing a poem
- Take a photo of something in nature
- Take a photo of yourself

- Limit your screen time to 1 hour

- 5-min stretching each morning

- Read a Bible verse

- Give someone a sincere compliment

- Share one positive quote on social media

- Floss

- Dance for 3 minutes

- Film your family one minute every day

- Complete a 10-minute weightlifting workout

- Write down three things you're excited about for the day

- Take 10 minutes for a gratitude meditation

- Cook something from a different cuisine each day

- Memorize a scripture or quote

- Spend 10 minutes working on a DIY project

- Create a daily goal list with your top three priorities

- Eat a vegetable each day

- Write and send a handwritten letter to a friend or family member (100 to one person or 100 to different people)

- Learn and practice a new magic trick for 10 minutes

- Organize and declutter a small part of your digital files

- Practice 10 minutes of public speaking or presentation skills

- Take a 15-minute walk in a different neighborhood each day

- Experiment with a new hairstyle or grooming technique

- Spend 5 minutes working on a puzzle or brain teaser

- Try a new type of food

- Put away your phone 1 hour before bed

- Be asleep by 10pm & get 8 hours of sleep a night

- Play a card or board game with your family
- Commit to 10 minutes of mindful coloring or doodling
- Try a new form of exercise or fitness class each day
- Learn about a historical event or figure for 10 minutes
- Write and share a daily fun fact or trivia
- Spend 10 minutes on a craft project
- Track your spending on a spreadsheet
- Do 10 minutes of gardening
- Listen to a new type of music genre or artist each day
- Learn and practice basic origami for 10 minutes
- Spend 15 minutes practicing photography with your smartphone
- Watch a 10-minute TED Talk or educational video
- Learn a new word in a foreign language and use it in a sentence
- Write a daily poem or creative piece of writing
- Try a new type of art medium or technique each day
- Learn about a new culture or tradition for 10 minutes
- Write down a joke to share with others
- Spend 10 minutes on self-care or a pampering ritual
- Give your kid/s an 8-second hug
- Tell someone "I love you"
- Run a mile a day
- Train for a long race
- Recycle something each day

Circle five goals on the list that interest you. Then take the top three and write them down. What excites or draws you toward these particular goals? Why? Select ONE to focus on for the next 100 days.

THE
5 C's
OF SUCCESS

1. COMMIT

2. CALENDAR

3. CHEERLEADER

4. CONSISTENCY

5. CUTOFF

The 5 C's

COMMIT: WRITE IT DOWN

Researchers studied Harvard MBA students before graduation and asked them, "Have you set clear, written goals for your future and made plans to accomplish them?"

They found that 84% of students had no goals set, 13% had goals in mind but didn't write them down, and only 3% had goals written on paper along with clear plans to accomplish them.

Ten years passed, and the researchers checked back in with the graduates and discovered that the abstract goal setters were making twice the amount of money as the students who had set no goals. Impressive, right?

But the real success story was in the 3% who had written their goals; they were making TEN TIMES the income of the other 97% <u>combined</u>.

The 3% who had written their goals were making TEN TIMES the income of the other 97% combined.

Who doesn't want to make TEN TIMES MORE than the average human?!

The secret? Write down your goals!

Be part of the 3% who make TEN TIMES MORE by writing down your goal that you have committed to. A goal is a wish unless it's written down.

WRITE YOUR COMMITMENT:

I, _____, commit to _____ for 100 days, beginning _____ and ending _____.

What inspired you to set this
particular goal?

DANICA CONTOR (D.C. CONTOR): 100 DAYS OF WRITING

I've been a storyteller all my life, and it's shown up in writing. I used to write daily, spending hours and hours on plotlines and character backgrounds. Then I had kids. My brain was too tired to figure out plot holes, and I certainly did not have the time to spend hours on anything (other than nursing), so I stopped writing.

Years passed and more babies were born. Then one day Kelli posted her 1 Goal for 100 Days challenge to choose one thing and do it for 100 days. Well, my brain immediately wanted to write, but then the voices started, "But you don't have time, you don't have hours, you don't even have a brain left!" So I decided to make it stupid-easy: one word. That was my marker. One word counted as writing. I could do that. I could write one single word every day for 100 days.

> *I realized I had been putting crazy conditions on what "counted" as writing when the reality was it all counted. One word counted.*

I traced 100 little boxes on some graph paper. Then, I did it. Most days I wrote way more, but there were days where I literally wrote "she said" as my word count for the day, and I was good with that. No judgment.

That one challenge jump-started my writing again. I realized I had been putting crazy conditions on what "counted" as writing when the reality was it all counted. One word counted.

Now, almost four years later, I've plotted out my five-book young adult contemporary fantasy series, and the first one comes out in May!

The 5 C's

COMMIT: GO PUBLIC!

One of the best ways to keep yourself accountable is to share your goal publicly. It's easy to let *yourself* down, but when you share your commitment with a friend or family member you are more likely to do it because you don't want to let *them* down.

Psychologist Benjamin Hardy highlights this phenomenon:

"As psychological research has found, when you make a public commitment, you will feel a sense of social pressure to be consistent with what you've said. Additionally, you'll get multiple other people committed. It's not willpower that's driving you, but external pressure, which pressure you've purposefully engineered because it forces you to achieve your goals."

I've noticed a pattern that the women who did 1 Goal for 100 Days AND shared it publicly on social media were often the same ones who stuck with it the entire 100 days! Those who shared a countdown or regular updates on social media usually ended up completing all 100 days.

Tell the world about the 1 goal you've committed to for the next 100 days! Tag me @kellifrance and use the hashtag #1goalfor100days along the way. I'd love to see your journey unfold and reshare it.

If you're not a fan of social media, share your goal with a few close friends.

Continue to share your experience throughout the 100 days to let your friends, fam, and fans know how it's going! This will help keep you even more accountable and allow others to cheer you on. Plus, you might just inspire someone along the way.

Share your goal on social media! What were some of the most meaningful responses you received? How did these responses impact your motivation and commitment?

BECKI WHITBECK: 100 DAYS AT THE GYM

I don't finish things. At least, that was the story I told myself. It felt like the recurring theme of my life. So deciding to take on a 100-day challenge to go to the gym everyday was a big deal.

I consistently shared my journey publicly on social media, updating what day I was on. About 50 days into the challenge, someone in the neighborhood stopped me in the street and said that I was doing great. "You've inspired me!" That was the first time I realized I could inspire someone I didn't really know, and that people were watching me. It definitely incentivised me to keep going. People were watching! But more than that, I didn't want to give up on myself like I have many times in my life.

I started taking the classes offered at the gym. I discovered that I could lift weights throughout the class or survive cardio for 55 min straight. My instructors knew me and remembered my name—the best feeling in the world. I felt seen.

> I ended up doing another 100 days with another goal because after the first round, I realized that I can do ANYTHING for 100 days!

I have gained strength beyond building muscles. I now have a community at the gym with, like-minded people who connect for that one hour each week. I receive messages from people on social media who I didn't even know were watching me or that I haven't talked to in 20 years. It's absolutely amazing how sharing one little thing can inspire so many people.

I am able to actively play with my kids longer, my clothes fit better, and I can move furniture around my house without a fear of injury. But it's honestly the time to myself to get centered every day and the self confidence I've gained that have been my biggest wins.

More than that, I'm proud of the fact that I committed to something and FINISHED it.

The 5 C's

CALENDAR: PUT IT ON YOUR SCHEDULE

I often consult with new entrepreneurs looking for advice. They tell me all about WHAT their new ideas are and WHY they are so passionate about them. But when I ask WHEN they plan to work on them, they are at a total loss.

WHEN—what time and what days—do you plan to work on this business?

If you are really serious about taking action towards achieving your goal, then you need to determine the WHEN. Put it on your schedule. A goal is just a wish unless it's scheduled on your calendar.

The key to getting what you want in life is being intentional, especially with your time. Being intentional requires planning and scheduling in advance.

One morning as I drove my teenage son to school, I asked him what his plans were. It was Halloween and he wanted to do something super fun, but he still didn't have official plans. Like any good mom, I gave him some unsolicited advice: If you fail to plan, you plan to fail.

It's a life lesson that I continue to learn: in order to get what you want or have the experiences you want, you have to plan and schedule them. Planning and scheduling are a must. I truly believe this! I encouraged him to make a bucket list of fun things he wanted to do as a teenager and then assign them a certain weekend.

IF YOU FAIL TO PLAN, YOU PLAN TO FAIL.

If you have a goal to walk every day, pick a certain time and put it on your calendar. It can be the same time everyday or it can be scheduled on your calendar week by week. Block off a specific time to work on it.

You can't just sit around and wait for your dream life to fall into your lap. You have to plan it and put it on the calendar to make your goals happen.

Write down all the things going on in
your week. Look for the open spaces.
Where can you find a set time to work
on your goals?

_____

_____

_____

_____

_____

_____

_____

_____

_____

_____

_____

_____

_____

_____

_____

_____

HEATHER ENGLAND: 100 DAYS OF A CLEAN KITCHEN SINK

When Kelli challenged us to stick to a goal for 100 days, I thought hard about what stresses me the most. Because I have seven kids, I knew my goal would be about housework. The spot in our house that is always a nuisance is the kitchen. We walk through it every time we leave or come home. Each morning I am greeted by a dirty dish pile that just keeps growing.

So I challenged myself to have a clean sink each night before I go to bed. The first few weeks were rough. There were nights that we didn't get home until 10:00 pm, or dinner didn't even get started until 9:00 pm due to all of the kids' activities. The first few weeks were rough. I wanted so badly to go to bed when the rest of my family did. I wanted to ignore the dishes like we usually do because we were exhausted. But I was determined. Day 1 turned into 10, which turned into 50, and then 100!

> *Shockingly enough, the task got easier as the days went on.*

I can't lie, there were several nights I wanted to cry or give up because I needed sleep or there were ten other things that needed to be done instead. But I turned on music, blocked out my negative thoughts, and went to work. Shockingly enough, the task got easier as the days went on.

I made it! No dishes in the sink when I went to bed for 100 days, but it didn't stop there. Even now, I'm still in the habit of my goal! I start my day off on a high note, seeing my empty sink as I walk out the door to begin my busy day.

The 5 C's

CHEERLEADER: GET AN ACCOUNTABILITY PARTNER

One of the best ways to stay consistent with your goals is to get another person involved. I call this person an Accountability Partner. This might be someone who's doing the goal alongside you or someone you simply report to. Pearson's Law states that "When performance is measured, performance improves. When performance is measured and reported back, the rate of improvement accelerates."

> *"Most people avoid accountability because most people are not committed to their dreams. Instead, they're committed to their excuses." -Benjamin Hardy*

The American Society of Training and Development found that people are 65% more likely to achieve a goal after committing to another person.

To find a partner, start by asking close family or friends if any of them would be interested in doing the same goal with you. If that doesn't work, put out the word on social media. You could say something like, "I'm thinking about doing X for the next 100 days. Is there anyone who wants to be my Accountability Partner and do it with me?"

> *Studies show that people are 65% more likely to achieve a goal after committing to another person.*

You'll be surprised by the new friends you'll make when you reach out to find an Accountability Partner. Being accountable to a common goal or interest for 100 days tends to bond people.

Several years ago, My Mom was looking for a walking partner. One day, as she sat in a salon chair getting her hair done, the stylist mentioned that her mom, Pam, was the most non-judgemental person she knew. That piqued my mom's interest. I know this might sound weird, but could I get Pam's number? She reached out soon after and asked Pam to be her walking partner.

They have been walking together almost every morning for seven years now! Their beautiful friendship has grown substantially, all because my mom needed an Accountability Partner. Imagine the future friends you might make by being courageous and reaching out to find your own Pam.

DAY

7

Make a list of potential accountability partners. Write down what you'll say when you ask one of them to be your Partner. Then be brave and ask. Get ready for Future Friends to come into your life!

AMANDA LEX: RAN ONE MILE FOR 100 DAYS

I have been following Kelli France for the past three years as a coach, mentor, and friend. I admired her fearlessness, positive mindset, and willingness to share her journey with the world. When she started talking about this 100 day challenge, it inspired me to get on board. I started my 100 day journey on January 1st. I always wanted to be a runner. I was never good at it, and I envied my friends who talked about how wonderful and freeing running was for them. That morning, the first of the year, I decided to commit to running one mile every day for 100 days.

I printed out the tracker (found at kellifrance.com/tracker) and started on the treadmill in the basement. In the beginning it was tough. As a mom of two, there was a lot of starting and stopping to go to the bathroom. My pelvic floor was weak and I was not prepared for that. I ran every morning. I was able to take my 14-minute mile down to 8 minutes in just 100 days. My pelvic floor got stronger, I lost 9 pounds, and I felt healthier and more confident. I noticed that when I was making time to run, I was also eating better and drinking less alcohol. I found myself wanting to run further distances and by the time the challenge was completed, I was running 4 miles a day.

> *By the time the challenge was completed, I was running **4** miles a day.*

The goal tracker helped to keep me accountable, and it was really satisfying crossing off those boxes every day. I also utilized my Facebook stories to document my runs and was told that I inspired other women to start their 100 day challenge as well. When my challenge ended, I started a Facebook group and encouraged others to join. Members would choose their goal, print their trackers, and we would post and encourage each other.

After I ran one mile for 100 days, I switched to doing 30 minutes of pilates every day. Some days I would also add in weights. I ended up doing 200 consistent days, losing 15 pounds and completely changing my body from the inside out.

The 100 day challenge has been such a great motivator for me. It's not easy, but it's so rewarding when you check off day 100 and see the results of your hard work.

The 5 C's

CHEERLEADER: WEEKLY ACCOUNTABILITY MEETINGS

If you really want to up your game and increase your chances of succeeding at your goal, you need to prioritize this one thing: Hold ongoing Accountability Meetings with your Accountability Partner.

Studies[1] show that having a specific accountability appointment with someone you've committed to increases your chances of success to 95 percent! 95% is an incredible rate! That's practically guaranteeing that you will accomplish your 100 day goal!

> *Studies show that having a specific accountability appointment with someone you've committed to increases your chances of success to 95 percent!*

Adding ongoing meetings with your Accountability Partner into your schedule is an incredibly effective way to keep yourself in check. You can keep these meetings simple by making them a quick call, text, or Zoom. You can even add in extra accountability by telling your Accountability Partner what to do if you don't respond or show up.

Weekly (or bi-weekly, or even daily) meetings are so effective because you set up a plan in place, in advance, for those times when you get discouraged, burned out, or unmotivated regarding your goals. And let's be honest, you WILL get discouraged, burned out, or unmotivated! That's why it's important to plan your strategy for those times that those feelings inevitably come up.

Weekly Accountability Meetings are something I did to help me write this very book. Every Friday, I had a Zoom call with my editor, Lacy. We would go over what I had written during the week. This ongoing, scheduled system helped me stay on track with my writing goals. It was a GAME-CHANGER for helping me write this book in 100 days!

---

[1] The American Society of Training and Development

How often do you want to check in with your partner and why? What format (text, call, Zoom, in-person) will you use to connect? Brainstorm what you want these meetings to look like.

AMY AMSPOKER: 100 DAYS OF DEEP BREATHING

I tend to get easily overwhelmed with everything going on in life and react quickly without fully processing things. And before I began this challenge, I certainly had a lot to process! Deep breathing allowed me to slow down and gave me some quiet time to reflect and react to things more positively.

About 6 months before the challenge, my medical mystery started. I'd been going from specialist to specialist to try to figure out what's going on with some of my lab work, but each time results would be unhelpful or inconclusive. Because of these unexplained and abnormal lab results, I was unable to get life insurance from any companies. I really wanted to give up, but knew I owed it to my family and myself to keep looking for an answer.

> *This one little practice has truly been a life changer for me.*

When I finally learned that I most likely had thyroid cancer, I found that engaging in purposeful deep breathing had a huge impact on the way I processed my diagnosis and experience. It enabled me the time and space to reflect, pray, and just be. Prior to deep breathing I used to get so overwhelmed by my emotions that I would just freeze. I was paralyzed and could not move forward.

After consciously practicing deep breathing for 100 days, my mental health is in a better place than it has ever been before—which surprises me, given the complexity of my life right now. I feel comfortable, confident, and even somewhat empowered. It's enabled me to be able to make ALL of the appointments and connect with those I need to connect with. It's been a rough year, but this one little practice has truly been a life changer for me. Staying consistent with this challenge helped me carry the practice beyond the 100 days.

The 5 C's

BE YOUR OWN CHEERLEADER ("GO ME!")

One day several years ago, when I picked up my youngest son from preschool, I found everyone playing the game "Duck, Duck, Goose". His preschool friends begged me to play with them, so I joined in. I can't turn down adorable preschoolers.

We all sat criss-cross applesauce in a circle on the rug, eagerly anticipating when the person standing would tap our head and yell "Goose!"

The first time my son got picked as the goose, he ran around the circle and yelled out, "GO, ME! GO, ME!" It was so cute and fascinating to witness. Every time he got tagged, he continued to yell out, "GO, ME! GO, ME!" to cheer himself on as he ran towards his goal.

That day, my son inspired me to strive harder to be my own best cheerleader.

His boisterous self-encouragement got me thinking how I wish more women would say "GO ME!" to themselves more often. As a Confidence Coach, I often see women being the harshest critics of themselves, belittling their own accomplishments or potential.

As women we have enough harsh critics in the world. We don't need to be that for ourselves! Besides, we won't get as far if we are constantly chanting personal put-downs along the way.

We all need encouragement, especially when we are working towards a greater goal. The word "encourage" has the word "courage" in it. And that's what happens when we en-courage ourselves, we give ourselves courage to move forward.

So be like Max – be your own cheerleader, yelling "GO ME! GO ME" on your journey.

If you don't cheer yourself on, who will?

What are some ways you can cheer
yourself on in this journey?

TRISHA REYNOLDS: COLD-WATER THERAPY FOR 100 DAYS

After finishing this challenge, I think I'll just keep going, probably forever. I took a cold shower everyday for 100 days. Usually it was 2 minutes but sometimes it was longer and sometimes it was a bath. I missed a few days while I was out camping with no shower access, but I made sure to double up when I got home to "make up" for it.

I had toyed around with cold water therapy in the past, but never with this level of consistency. The challenge helped me push through on the hard days and just get it done. I have benefitted in MANY ways from doing this consistently. The other day I went to the doctor and my SpO2 (blood oxygen) was 100%. The medical assistant was shocked and said he's never seen that. Turns out it's one of the many benefits of cold showers.

> *I think I'll just keep going, probably forever.*

I used to always feel cold throughout the day but my body temperature is much better regulated now. I like to watch my heart rate when I'm in the shower. After about 30 or 45 seconds in the cold, my heart rate drops by 20-25 BMPs. Our bodies are so powerful! Cold showers give you a 250% increase in dopamine. It's like a natural antidepressant. I could go on and on about the benefits. Thanks for the kick start!

DAY

12

The 5 C's

CONSISTENCY: SEINFELD SAYS

Goals are hard at the start, messy in the middle, and worth it at the end. Consistency is the Messy Middle. It's the not-so-glamourous part of reaching success. It's the boring steps on the ladder. The focus on one foot in front of the other.

The messy middle is what matters.

> *"The messy middle is what matters." -Kelli France*

An aspiring comic once asked Jerry Seinfeld for advice after a show. Seinfeld told him the only way to get better at telling jokes was to write them every day. He told the young comic to get a calendar and mark an X for every day he wrote jokes. He said:

"After a few days you'll have a chain. Just keep at it and the chain will grow longer every day. You'll like seeing that chain, especially when you get a few weeks under your belt. Your only job is to not break the chain."

I've had thousands of women take my 1 Goal for 100 Days challenge and what I've noticed is that those who do it in a row, and don't break the chain, are the most successful. Momentum is a powerful force!

However, don't let missing one day buck you off entirely. This is the 100 Day Challenge! Not the 100-Day-In-a-Row Challenge. If you miss a day (or two days or ten days), simply continue on. You're not resetting back to zero, but carrying on from wherever you left off.

If you haven't yet, download & print the
100-Day Tracker at
www.kellifrance.com/tracker

When have you experienced the power of
maintaining a streak or a chain in your life?
How long did you last? What broke the chain
and what can you learn from that?

MICHELLE BEHRENDT: 100 DAYS OF LANGUAGE LESSONS

After five plus years of Spanish classes in school that I barely remember, I wanted to see if I could get reengaged with learning a language. I also wanted my goal to be something that wasn't part of my normal day. I had sporadically tried to do some lessons before but never stuck with it. I decided to do 100 days of language lessons every day using the Duolingo app.

It was a struggle some days to do the minimum one lesson and the app would send me all sorts of alerts trying to remind me to practice. Other days I would get into it and do a whole bunch of lessons.

> *The more days of successful completion I had, I realized I didn't want to lose my streak.*

But the more days of successful lesson completion I had, I realized I didn't want to lose my streak. **I have now done over 300 days** (as of this writing) and I am really quite proud of that accomplishment!!!

I have a long way to go to being fluent, but have recognized some basic words out in the world, which feels so amazing. It's something that has become part of my daily habits and I'm excited to continue my language learning.

The 5 C's

CUTOFF: DEADLINES DISTRACT US FROM FEAR

One of the best ways to overcome perfectionism and overwhelm is to implement deadlines as mile markers along the way. Deadlines are effective and powerful because they distract us from fear. Deadlines can positively avert our attention from discomfort, the fear of failure, and not being good enough—uncertainties we're programmed to run away from.

Having a deadline makes us stop thinking about whether we should do the work, and forces us to actually do it. It pushes us out of our head and into action. Instead of running away from the work, the deadline initiates us to run towards the work.

Deadlines give us a sense of urgency to expedite our efforts. Deadlines help us focus and eliminate distractions. As I write this, I have a pending deadline that has forced me to cancel unnecessary items on my calendar that might take time away from writing this book. Creating my own self-imposed deadlines helps me prioritize the task at hand.

Deadlines are also effective because they create clarity on what is expected and when. When confusion is eliminated, performance is elevated.

"When confusion is eliminated, performance is elevated." -Kelli France

Deadline also help us divide larger tasks into smaller, more manageable components. I recommend breaking your 100 Day Goal into seven or ten ten-day chunks. Knowing that you have to do a task for only seven or ten days makes it feel less intimidating.

There can be a dark side to deadlines if they cause you too much anxiety or stress. Make sure that the deadlines you create are realistic ones that you can succeed at.

How can you implement deadlines or
milestone markers to boost your focus,
productivity, and confidence?

RACHEL ANGLE : 100 DAYS OF WALKING ONE MILE OUTSIDE

I was in a slump until Kelli issued the 100 Days Challenge. I felt down and unmotivated in every area of my life! I was skipping workouts and eating poorly. My business was stagnating because I wasn't feeling great about myself. My personal growth was backsliding.

But I knew from past experience that the endorphins I get when I move my body and exercise make me a happy person. I knew that if I walked just one mile outside in nature and fresh air everyday, I would feel more energized, happy, and could channel that energy into all areas of my life.

> *Walking a mile every day changed my mindset, physical health, and life-perspective.*

And it did! Making the commitment to move outside every day (rain or shine) really helped to center me. There is an undeniable power to the outdoors. I honestly feel like walking a mile every day changed my mindset, physical health, and life-perspective. It's incredible to me that such a small thing could have such a huge impact! I can't emphasize how important this was to my success.

Of course, it wasn't easy. There were definitely days I wanted to skip. But one thing that kept me going was accountability with friends who were doing their own version of the 100-Day Challenge.

I know that exercise might not energize everyone the same way it does for me. However, I highly recommend that you find something that does energize you and implement it into your daily life. No matter what you choose, it will have a positive impact on your life!

STRATEGIES
FOR
STARTING

1. START SMALL

2. START SLOW

3. START SLOPPY

4. SET YOURSELF UP FOR SUCCESS

5. SET YOURSELF UP FOR SETBACKS

START SMALL

Now that you've narrowed down to one goal, I want you to close your eyes and imagine yourself doing it everyday for 100 days. Does it seem doable?

Your dreams may be enormous, but to succeed, your goal should start super small. Sticking to one, bite-size, actionable daily goal will build momentum and set you up for success.

If you plan to do something each day for 30 minutes, I suggest you cut the time down to 5 mins. Do you plan to write a chapter a day? Set it for a page a day instead. Planning to send 30 messages a day? Make it 3.

Of course, you may want to do more (and maybe you will end up doing more!) but you also need to minimize it so that if you're having a crazy day, you can still squeeze it in. It's not a go-big-or-go-home challenge. It's a stay-sustainable-and-stay-in challenge.

What adjustments can you make to break your goal down into a bite-size daily action? How might this smaller daily commitment make the goal seem more achievable and sustainable in your daily life?

"You don't have to be great to start, but you have to start to be great."

— ZIG ZIGLAR

LAURALYNE NEWBOLD CHORD: 100 DAYS OF MAKING THE BED

I chose what I considered a simple goal, not really comprehending the impact it would have in my life. My goal was to make my bed every day. So simple, right? But the surprise was, it gave me a nudge to do more!

I felt empowered to do more throughout my day.

I found myself seeing the nightstand beside my bed and straightening that too! I felt empowered to do more throughout my day. I got a second bedspread and changed my sheets more regularly.

Every time I walked into my room, I loved seeing my bed all beautiful! It made me smile. When I smiled my mood was boosted. Filling my calendar with stickers was super motivating for me, too. It was a win, win, win all the way around!

START SLOW (WITH ORIENTATION WEEK)

Any time we start something new, it's going to feel uncomfortable. We might think we're doing something wrong, but we're not! We're merely getting oriented! With any new transition, you're leaving your comfort zone and need some time to settle in to your New Normal.

Most colleges require incoming freshmen to attend an Orientation Week. They do this because they understand how dis-orienting it can be for young adults to move to a new place, live away from home for the first time, and start a new course of study. Orientation Week usually includes a series of acclimating events that help a first-year student explore and adjust to this new beginning.

When starting a new goal, we need to Start Slow and give ourselves an Orientation Week (or two!) to adjust to this new experience. Orientation Week allows you to try out your new goal with grace. It is a buffer that gives us a chance to review and revise what's working and what is not. If we can give ourselves compassion during the beginning it will help us build momentum so that we won't be as likely to give up.

On a whim, my daughter and I signed up for the San Diego Half Marathon. It was going to take place two days after our shared birthday (my 40th and her 18th—big milestones!) and we thought it would be a cool way to celebrate together. For the record, we were NOT fast or frequent runners. It was waaaaay out of our comfort zones but we wanted to do it anyway. One last bonding adventure together before Savannah moved out!

After a week or so of going on super long runs together, we both realized something: we didn't actually want to run the half-marathon! The time required to prepare and train was so much more than either of us wanted to invest in running. Heck, we didn't even like running! We just thought the idea of running a half-marathon on our shared birthday sounded awesome. But in reality, it was not something we actually wanted to do.

So we both happily quit and ended up going on a trip to New York City to see the Rockettes and the giant Christmas tree at the Rockefeller Center instead. It turned out to be a much more enjoyable way to celebrate for us!

The point of this story is that sometimes you need a week or so to figure out what you DON'T want to do. Some things sound better in theory than they turn out in practice. Consider your first week of the 100 Days your Orientation Week and allow yourself extra grace as you find your bearings (and maybe even swap out your goal).

What have you learned so far in your 100 day journey? What adjustments can you make to improve your experience?

"Patience, persistence and perspiration make an unbeatable combination for success."

- NAPOLEON HILL

DAY

21

MIMI ABRAHAM: 100 DAYS OF CLOSING HER WATCH RINGS

Nothing has changed my perspective on fitness more than when I was diagnosed with Multiple Sclerosis a few years ago. Since then I have researched and tried different forms of exercises and vitamins in hopes that the benefits will slow down my progression of this debilitating disease. I invested in an Apple Watch this past July and set a 100-Day goal to close my three fitness rings each day: Movement, Exercise, and Standing.

> *I have even been able to stop two different medications.*

Working at a desktop and constantly fighting the fatigue that comes with MS, it's so important to me to keep my body from being stagnant. It wasn't always easy. There were MANY days that I had to push through and get it done, but I did it. I have even been able to stop two different medications. I often do yoga and pilates and plenty of times do the modified version, but I feel my body stronger and my mind more at peace.

Strategies for Starting

START SLOPPY

Are you a Perfectionist Procrastinator? As women, we tend to wait until everything is perfect before we put something out there.

When I launched my Finally Fearless podcast, there were a LOT of things that were not ready. There were also a ton of things that were ready...but not perfect. It was a hot mess!

Ten minutes before we planned to launch, I messaged my podcast team and said "Will the podcasts all be ready in the next 10 minutes like we planned?" They wrote back and told me that only one of the three episodes launching had been approved by Apple. UGH. The other 3 episodes weren't approved yet.

There was so much left to do. The web page wasn't ready. The audio graphics weren't ready. We hadn't even started the newsletter. Deep breaths. Instead, I gave myself and my podcast team a deadline and we made it happen...imperfectly.

If I would've waited until it was perfect, it wouldn't have happened. Perfect isn't always possible. Sloppy is.

80% is better than 0% so start before you're ready! You can fix it as you go but first you've got to START!!! You'll never win if you don't begin so stop being a perfectionist procrastinator and start before you're ready.

Put on those workout shoes (even if they're 10 years old).

Publish that first blog post (even if you're unsure of the spelling).

Book that first client (even if it's your sister).

Make that phone call (even if you don't know what you're going to say).

Just do it (even if you suck).

Start Sloppy.

What's one thing you will start
IMPERFECTLY in the next
24 hours?

You don't need to have confidence in your ability to do something. You just need confidence in your ability to figure it out.

JODY JANSSEN: 100 DAYS OF NO SODA

I had slipped into a state of grabbing a Dr. Pepper as a crutch anytime I got stressed, anxious, happy, or sad. No matter what I was feeling, that was my go-to. At the same time, I was battling high blood pressure issues and I had been trying to lose some extra weight, with zero success. I was frustrated, and realized that giving up soda was something that could at least help me a little bit.

At first, it was very much a decision that I had to constantly remind myself I had made. I didn't realize how much stopping at the convenience store every time I went through town had become a habit. I also didn't realize how dependent I had become on that caffeine and sugar rush. I found myself looking for excuses to run to town just so I could grab a Dr. Pepper, but then stopped myself.

I was sabotaging myself by allowing my emotions to serve as a reason to indulge in something I knew was bad for me. Completing this goal made me realize that even the most seemingly insignificant things can make a huge difference in the grand scheme of my life. I was reminded that I could set and reach goals. I was reminded that I could say no to something I really liked for my own benefit. That was the beginning of a healthier me.

> Completing this goal made me realize that even the most seemingly insignificant things can make a huge difference in the grand scheme of my life.

Should this have been a hard goal to complete? Probably not. Was it? Yeah, some days it really was. But I did it and I did it despite my friends telling me, "Oh, one soda won't hurt you." I did it despite my kids offering to pick up a soda for me or asking if I wanted to share a soda with them. I did it despite some days really not wanting to. When I think my goals are too big and too difficult, I tell myself that's okay and remind myself that I've already done things I didn't think I could do before.

While weight loss wasn't the goal, it has been a very happy side effect. More importantly, I feel so much better physically. And honestly, I'm so proud of myself for taking a stand for me, even if it was a stand against myself. Now, when I think about things I want to accomplish, whether in business or in life, I remind myself that I can do hard things.

Strategies for Starting

SET YOURSELF UP FOR SUCCESS

How can you set things up to support your goal to be as successful as possible? If I head out for the beach but forget my sunscreen, towel, and swimsuit, I probably won't last long there. In the same way, you want to make your goal as easy and achievable for yourself as possible.

What resources do you need to make it a success?

If you're already feeling overwhelmed, consider cutting your goal in half. Another great tool is to create physical reminders. Set alarms on your phone or schedule it on your calendar. Maybe you literally don't have enough time in your day. Consider waking up 15 minutes earlier.

Are you a checklist person? Download the tracker at www.kellifrance.com/tracker to track your progress. Remove temptations: If you're cutting out alcohol, give away all the wine bottles in your house. Make it easy: if you're heading to the gym in the morning, lay out your workout clothes the night before. Get the right tools: if you have a goal to paint every day, make sure you stock up on paintbrushes!

Lastly, get it out of the way! If possible, execute your goal first thing in the morning. The sooner you do something the better; the longer you wait the less likely it is to happen.

What can you do to set yourself up for success each day? What resources do you need to make this goal a success?

"You do not rise to the level of your goals. You fall to the level of your systems."

- JAMES CLEAR

Strategies for Starting

SET YOURSELF UP FOR SETBACKS

On every new adventure, there will be stop lights, traffic jams, road bumps, or detours. Guaranteed. Plan on it. Prepare for it. Comedian Lily Tomlin jokes, "The road to success is always under construction."

To set yourself up for the setbacks, you must outsmart your excuses. We all have our own favorite excuses or go-to justifications. Mine used to be "but my kids need me" (which is true, but in my case it was often just an excuse disguised as martyrdom).

"You can have results or excuses. Not both." -Arnold Schwarzenegger

What are some of your favorite excuses? Maybe it's that it's too cold outside or you're traveling so you're not on your normal routine. Maybe it's that your kids are off from school or your home is being renovated so things feel too chaotic. People get very creative when coming up with excuses.

What are some of your go-to justifications? You know, the kind where we give ourselves a little too much grace to make us feel better about a mess-up or a moment of weakness. My go-to justification is "I'll do better tomorrow" or "I already messed up or missed a day so I might as well go big and give up." Grace is good until it enables us.

What temptations might come along throughout your journey? If you plan to do 100 days of no sugar, maybe the licorice in your pantry is just too tempting. If you plan to do 100 days of no alcohol, maybe hanging out in bars isn't the best idea.

Think ahead of all the excuses, justifications and temptations that might come your way during these 100 days. Then strategize some ways to eliminate them before they even happen.

What are some of your favorite excuses?
What are your go-to justifications? What
temptations might come your way? What
are some ways to eliminate these
obstacles?

THE HAIRBAND STOPPED HER: LEAH REMILLET'S STORY

I'm just not one of those people who enjoys exercise. I never have and I don't see that changing. Yet, I get that it's important and I want to be consistent. Key word…"want."

If I struggled at all to find my workout clothes in the morning, I was done. My warm bed was way too enticing. Then later in the day, I'd be disappointed because I really did want to exercise regularly so that I would have more energy and feel better.

So the next night I made sure I found all of my workout clothes and had them all setup. My shoes, socks, leggings, sports bra, t-shirt, all of it was there, stacked and ready for me. And that worked for a few days. Until one day I couldn't find a hair tie. And so back to bed I went— because 6-AM-me will find any reason not to do my workout. My bed was too warm and enticing. And so I didn't do a workout that day.

But then, of course later, I was disappointed once again because I didn't get the workout in. But here's the thing: I don't beat myself up over it, and I don't decide this is proof that I'll never be successful. Instead I see each block as a fence. I walk up to that fence and find a way to build a new gate so I can keep going. So, the very next day not only did I have the shoes, the socks, the leggings, the sports bra, and the t-shirt but I had a hair tie on the very top.

Progress will never happen if we think we need to be perfect! Progress happens when we keep showing up!

DAY

29

REVERSE ENGINEER YOUR GOALS

As moms, we are so good at reverse-engineering our time. We think, "Okay, if I have to be at my son's soccer game by 6 pm, then that means we need to leave by 5:40, which means we need to eat at 5:00 pm, which means I need to start cooking dinner by 4:30". You can do this same thing with your goals.

STEPS TO REVERSE ENGINEERING YOUR GOALS:

1. I want to go from _____ to _____ by _____
    (Needs a number and a date so that it's measurable)

2. Break it down by doing the math

3. What are some mile markers so I'll know I'm on my way?

4. What is a daily habit I can commit to to achieve this goal?

5. When will I work on this daily habit? (exact time each day)

6. What am I willing to sacrifice in order to make this a daily habit?

EXAMPLE:

I'll share how I reverse engineered my goals for finishing this book:

1. I want to go from having no pages written to having my book available on Amazon by the end of the year (in time for everyone's New Year's Resolutions).

2. I have 100 days to complete my goal and I want my book to be 100 pages long so I need to write 1 page per day.

3. Milestones: Finish writing two months before my deadline. Finish edits one month before my deadline. Finish design/formatting prep 15 days before my deadline.

4. Write 1 page everyday.

5. Write for 20 minutes every morning.

6. Sacrifice waking up earlier to get it done

Just like you get your kids to soccer on time, Breaking down the timeframe of your goal will increase your chances of achieving it substantially!

Your turn! Use these 6 steps to reverse
engineer your goal.

Always ask yourself if what you're doing today is getting you closer to where you want to be tomorrow.

INNER MEAN GIRL

You know that voice in your head that says cruel critical things out of nowhere? That's your Inner Mean Girl. She's your Brain Bully, your Inner Critic. She's like a really annoying roommate that follows you around whispering words of doubt and mean messages. She shows up to terrorize you when you least expect it, attacking you as you drive into town or blow-dry your hair.

Your Inner Mean Girl does not want you to grow or level up. So during this 100-day journey, she will try to stop you with every possible trick in the book. Some of her favorite tricks are Shoulding *"You should be doing it like this"), Comparison ("You're not doing as good as her"), All-or-Nothing Thinking ("If you can't do it perfectly, don't do it at all") & Mindreading ("Amy probably thinks I'm weird for doing this").*

Psychologist Rubin Khoddam says, "Your mind will constantly try to steer you away from committed action by saying things like, "I'll do it later" or "I'll have more time tomorrow." Your mind will try to tell you, "You can't do it" or "You're not good enough." However, those are all tricks. The funny thing about the mind is that it doesn't stop talking. Taking action may seem impossible until you actually do it."

It's time to kick out this unwanted roommate who's living rent-free in your head. She is taking away your power. One of the first steps to getting rid of her is to recognize her. Most people don't even realize they have an Inner Critic because they've spent years believing the lies she tells them. Start by writing down all the negative things she says in one day. You can even name her if that helps you to recognize those thoughts better. I named mine Lucy Fir ("Not today Lucy Fir!")

You will be shocked at how many mean things your Brain Bully says to you in one day! When you see your list, you might realize why you've been struggling or stuck. It's hard to move forward when you have all these negative thoughts pulling you back daily.

Having an Inner Mean Girl isn't the problem, it's our reaction to those critical thoughts that matters. We must react by rebelling. Our actions must be the opposite action from what our Inner Critic is trying to tell us not to do. In this case, it's your 1 Goal for 100 Days. Remember the commitment you made at the beginning. Remember why you started. Ignore your Inner Mean Girl. Take committed action to revolt against her! Keep going. Continue on in your 100-day journey. You're doing better than you think!

List all the things your Inner Mean Girl says to you in one day. Then write a manifesto against it. Channel your Inner Bestie. What does SHE think of you?

REWARD YOURSELF ALONG THE WAY

I told myself that after I wrote this essay, I could treat myself to a Diet Coke from McDonalds and stop at Target to browse…alone. Mmmm, nothing is better! And guess what? It's working! I am sticking to my goal of writing this page and I am doing it very quickly and without distraction because I have a reward at the end that I'm working toward.

The promise of even a small reward can be a powerful carrot to keep you plodding forward, especially on the difficult days. Of course, the true rewards are keeping promises to yourself, practicing consistency, or forming a habit you've always dreamed of! But meanwhile, it doesn't hurt to treat yourself for good behavior.

Maybe you take yourself shopping alone at the end of each successful 10 days. Grab a fun drink from your favorite café, read for an uninterrupted hour, light candles around your bath, buy makeup online, take a cat nap, or watch day-TV. Choose something you normally don't allow yourself and hook it to the accomplishment of your goal—whether daily, weekly, or monthly.

At the end of the 100 days, you may want to mark out a larger reward.

After completing this challenge, I'll…

Book that vacation

Get a massage

Take a day off

Host a celebration party

Take my family out to a nice dinner

Buy the shoes

Donate to charity

Even though you're keeping your goal small and manageable, the 100-Day challenge is still that—a challenge! Remember to pat yourself on the back for a job well done. And now I'm heading off to Target! Byeeeee!

What will you reward yourself with? Brainstorm five rewards— big and small—that might help keep you motivated.

"Don't cheat yourself, treat yourself."

– DWAYNE JOHNSON

LEAH REMILLET: 100 DAYS OF FAMILY HISTORY

I decided to do the 1 Goal for 100 days Challenge in large part because I adore Kelli but also because I had set the goal for the new year to be more consistent in small habits. I thought this would be a really fun way to try to make that happen and it would add a layer of accountability that I knew I needed in order to be more successful!

The goal I chose was family history. I'm a total genealogy nerd. It's something that I have loved doing for years, but have not been inconsistent with. Some years, I research a lot of family history. Other years, months and months go by and I haven't picked it up or touched anything. The previous couple years have been like the latter, and I really wanted family history to be a part of my regular life again.

> *I'm on day 352 and I have no intentions of stopping.*

One obstacle I often face when goal setting is that I go too big. Then I find myself in all-or-nothing thinking, and I end up on the nothing end of the spectrum when my goal isn't sustainable. However, this time I came up with a simple system to make it easy to do family history each day. My system was to go into my family tree app, search out one task, and do that task everyday. My favorite is when the task involves an opportunity to find a picture of an ancestor and add it to the tree. I love seeing their faces.

I didn't miss a single day, which felt so good! The 1 Goal for 100 Days set me on a path to feeling and believing that I am a person who shows up consistently. And the more days in a row I hit, the more I didn't want to break the chain. In fact, as of this morning, I'm on day 308 of doing family history every single day and I have no intentions of stopping.

YOU'RE NOT AN IMPOSTOR, YOU'RE A BEGINNER

Imposter Syndrome is not really a syndrome at all. Reshma Saujani, bestselling author of *Brave, Not Perfect*, speaks brilliantly about this fallacy in a recent commencement speech. She tells the story of "Bike Face," a diagnosis doctors came up with in the late 1800's for women who rode bicycles. Back then, bikes were new and gaining popularity among women, but men didn't love the freedom it gave women.

Women diagnosed with Bike Face showed *"a litany of supposed symptoms, from 'flushed' cheeks and 'bulging eyes' to 'an expression either anxious, irritable, or at best…stony.' That's right: Before there was resting bitch face, there was resting bike face."*

Labeling the discomfort as "bike face" was an attempt to shove women who'd challenged the status quo back into a convenient, less-mobile, box. And for a moment, it worked.

"Impostor syndrome is based on the premise that we're the problem, but, in my experience, discomfort is a normal, human reaction to my environment."

Reshma Saujani urges us to challenge the term, "impostor syndrome," which she declares as "just a tool—to keep our concentration on our own inadequacies."

Our use of the term "Imposter Syndrome" is as silly as the "medical" diagnosis of Bike Face. Both terms label the natural process of being a beginner as unnatural, instead of embracing the very normal, very natural, discomfort that comes with any new challenge.

Next time you catch yourself with so-called "Imposter Syndrome", remind yourself that you are not an Impostor, you're a Beginner. Instead of saying "I am BAD" at something you just started, try saying "I am NEW." Allow yourself to be a Beginner and recognize that beginnings are often uncomfortable until they become as easy as… riding a bike.

Think about a time you've experienced feelings of self-doubt, especially when starting something new. How did these feelings manifest and what was your internal dialogue like? Now, consider the concept of reframing these thoughts from "I am BAD" to "I am NEW." How does this transform your perspective?

"Don't let the noise of others' opinions drown out your own inner voice."

- STEVE JOBS

YOU CAN'T CHASE TWO RABBITS

Did you know that 92% of New Year's Resolutions fail within a week of starting them? A big reason for this is because we over-commit and overwhelm ourselves.

As a teenager, I used to make HUGE lists of starry-eyed goals. I'd list several goals under separate categories: physical, intellectual, social, spiritual.

For physical, I would write:

- exercise 3 times a week

- drink more water

- eat more veggies

- go to bed by 10pm

- eat less junk food

And so on until I had about 20 wide-ranging goals. Can you guess how many I accomplished? None! It wasn't because I wasn't serious or ambitious enough. It was because I'd given myself too many things to focus on.

"If you chase two rabbits you will lose them both." -Confusius

Start thinking of goals as HABITS…or rabbits. You can only really create one habit at a time if you want it to stick. Confusius illustrated this when he said, "If you chase two rabbits, you will lose them both."

Anytime you use the word goal, replace it with the word habit (or even rabbit if that is a better visual). When you think of goals as habits you realize how unrealistic it is to create or change 20 habits at once, like I attempted as a teenager! You need to decide at the outset which rabbit to chase. Going after a singular habit (or rabbit-ha!) will be the most achievable and the least likely to overwhelm you or cause you to quit.

How will focusing on a single goal over 100 days impact your success and well-being?

CINDY LEWIS: 100 DAYS OF EATING KETO

In the beginning of the year, I decided that I wanted to get healthier. I challenged myself to 100 days of eating Keto. The first few weeks were the toughest. I had so many cravings and I also got what they call the "Keto flu." I happen to be a huge potato lover and have always been obsessed with my daily Dr Pepper, so it was really tough for me to completely take them out of my life for 100 days.

After the first month, my cravings lightened up but then towards the end they came back with a vengeance. It was frustrating to have gone so long without these things and have the cravings come back!

> *I'm not only doing this for myself; I'm doing this for my kids.*

Every day I would wake up and remind myself: "I'm not only doing this for myself; I'm doing this for my kids. My kids deserve a healthy mom." That thought was the one thing that kept me strong through the whole 100-day challenge.

I am so glad I stayed strong through it because I am proud to say I lost 45 pounds and went down two pants sizes in that time! I feel so much healthier! I have more energy and am able to play with my kids more.

I believe anybody can do what they set their minds to. I felt amazing when I finished with the challenge. If you stick to it, you're going to feel enormous pride and accomplishment.

DAY

39

YOUR FUTURE-FILTER

When trying to determine your goal, take a moment to get clarity. What do you want? Most people have the hardest time answering that question. However, until you get clear on what you want, you won't get it. Period. I always tell my kids that if they don't put something on the grocery list, I won't buy it for them. Same goes for you. If you don't know what you want and don't put it out there, you won't get it.

Decide where you want to be 1-10 years down the road. Think of your own funeral. What do you want people to say about you? What do you want to have accomplished by the end of your life? What are some things you have on your bucket list? What are some of the things that you have always wanted to do? If a desire continues to come to your mind, don't ignore it. That desire is your sign. It's time to do something about it. Do not spend another year procrastinating. Imagine where you would be next year if you start now.

You may not always know the exact steps that lead to the future you want and that's okay! One of my favorite quotes is from fashion designer, Diane von Furstenberg, who proclaimed, "I didn't really know what I wanted to do, but I knew the woman I wanted to become." Start showing up as the woman you want to become. Eventually you will become her!

Get clear on what you want and then go for it! Use your Future Filter as a guide to point you in the right direction. Be your future self now.

Put on your Future-Filter. Describe the
woman you want to become.

Vizualize your highest self and start showing up as her.

STEPHANIE EDWARDS: 100 DAYS OF MARKETING

I wanted to make progress in my business but was having trouble committing to the marketing that I knew would help me. I'm a perfectionist. I suffer from analysis paralysis and it holds me back. Would I be able to do it like I was supposed to? When would I fit it into my busy day? What if I couldn't do it exactly right? Because I didn't have a solid plan to answer these questions I never started the task.

Then Kelli issued the 1 Goal for 100 Days challenge. I'm competitive. If you offer a challenge, I'm going to accept it and give it my all! So I decided to make marketing my goal. I decided I would start sloppy and do it for 100 days.

> *It was messy in the beginning, but as the days went on I found a groove.*

It was messy in the beginning, but as the days went on I found a groove. I found a system that made it easier to fit it into my day and to accomplish the task. And I did it for 100 days!!

I saw growth in my business and myself. The best part was that I developed habits which freed up brain space to work on new things that will help me grow because I no longer have to do a bunch of thinking or planning to do that task. I just got it done.

You may not have it all figured out when you start, but just start with something! Make adjustments as you go and allow yourself to be changed.

GUARANTEED GOALS

What would you do if you knew you couldn't fail? Recently in my virtual Book Club with over 5,000 women, we read Jon Acuff's book, *All it Takes is a Goal*. In this book (and then later on my podcast) Jon shared a concept that blew my mind. He said there was a way to commit to and go after a goal in a way that guarantees you achieve it. When I read this I was like, "Sign me up! I would do ANY goal that had a guarantee that I would achieve it!"

He wrote, "How do I know, not just hope, that in the next twelve months I'm going to be physically stronger than I've been in the last ten years? Because if I do 150 Crossfit workouts this year, it will be impossible for me not to get into better shape. I haven't worked out with weights in ten years. Guess what will happen if I workout with them 150 times this year?"

Guaranteed Goals require math, not a miracle. For it to be a Guaranteed Goal, you must be able to measure it. That means there must be a number involved so you can track it and recognize when you accomplish it. Jon gave the example of being kind to his wife and kids. That is NOT measurable. But being kind to his wife and kids for 100 days is! Reading more books is not measurable, but reading a dozen books is.

I know I'm not the only one who has chosen a vague goal and began halfheartedly working on it only to get discouraged because I wasn't getting results.

This idea of planning and measuring your goals in a way that there's no way you could NOT achieve it changed everything for me! I started thinking of ways to make my goals a guarantee by breaking them down into smaller chunks, extending the deadline, or devoting more time to them.

If you're going to take the time and energy to go after a goal, you might as well ensure your success. If you take the time to really think through and plan your goal out, I truly believe that you can achieve any goal, guaranteed.

What would you set out to do if you
knew you couldn't fail? How can you go
after your goal in a way that will
guarantee your success?

"Procrastination is the most common manifestation of Resistance because it's the easiest to rationalize. We don't tell ourselves, "I'm never going to write my symphony." Instead we say, "I am going to write my symphony; I'm just going to start tomorrow"

- STEVEN PRESSFIELD,
THE WAR OF ART

MAREN CHASE: 100 DAYS OF NOT EATING AFTER 6 PM

Kelli has issued her 1 Goal for 100 Days challenge a few times in her Finally Fearless Community Facebook group. I've started with her a few times, but never quite made it to 100 days. This time felt different though. I needed a change in my life. A literal lifestyle change. I have been struggling with depression for a few years, and hearing Kelli say, "Nothing changes, if nothing changes," really flipped a switch in my mind and helped me persist in this goal.

> *I am still going strong towards my goal for over 350 days now!*

I chose intermittent fasting, because I have a complicated relationship with food. I was a chronic late-night snacker. An I-deserve-a-little-treat-after-dinner kind of gal, for sure. I had taken up intermittent fasting on and off before and really appreciated the structure it gave. So in the new year, I decided to go full speed ahead with it. For some reason, this time it didn't feel like "just" a New Year's resolution either. I felt like real change had to happen, and it had to be because I wanted it to. It had to work this time! I was committed!

Since I started this, it's changed my entire relationship with food and my late-night eating habits. I don't really have to think twice about it anymore; the habit has become part of my normal life. **If you're questioning if you should 1 goal for 100 days, definitely do it! If for no other reason other than to prove to yourself that you can keep a promise to yourself.** I am still going strong towards my goal for over 350 days now!

FAIL IT 'TIL YOU NAIL IT

We sat on our friends' boat, our necks dwarfed by our life jackets, listening to our friend give us a wakesurfing tutorial. His family had been wakesurfing for years. This was our family's first attempt. As they explained the logistics, they casually mentioned that it takes about twenty tries before you can actually get up on the surfboard. TWENTY TRIES?! What?!? What did we sign up for?

My husband and my four kids and I all have different skill-levels and experience with surfing. So some of us stood up on the surfboard after only a few tries and some of us took a whole lot more than that (I won't embarrass myself by telling you which category I fell into. Ahem). Eventually, with lots of learning and patience, we ALL stood up on the surfboard!

Why do so many of us expect to strike gold on our first attempt? The first time we try anything we should just plan to suck at it. Instead, we tend to beat ourselves up for not getting it right and then tell ourselves that we just weren't meant for whatever we just attempted.

You can't have success without failure. It's part of the process! So whyyyyy are we so afraid of it? It's not just that we are afraid of what people will think of us, although that's part of it. The real reason we are afraid of failure is because we want to avoid the negative feelings of shame that often flood us when we fail.

Instead of indulging in shame, detour to curiosity. **Failure is simply feedback.** It's a hurdle with a clipboard trying to coach you toward improvement. Instead of asking WHY, ask WHAT. Instead of "Why is this happening to me? Why can't I do as well as her? Why me?", ask yourself: "WHAT can I learn from this? What are some simple ways I can improve after having this experience?"

When you make a mistake, try to find the lesson in it. Avoid your Inner Mean Girl who tries to shame you. Shame tells you that you are bad. Curiosity tells you that you made a bad choice. Teach yourself by using curiosity, instead of terrorizing yourself by using shame.

"Anyone who has never made a mistake has never tried anything new." -Albert Einstein

Some people say that you only fail if you quit. But I disagree. **You only fail if you don't learn from it.** So fall off the surfboard 20 times. Use your failures as feedback, learn from them, and then fail it 'till you nail it!

Think about a time you felt like a failure.
WHAT did you learn from it? What are
some simple ways you could have
improved after having this experience?

Fail It 'Til You Nail It!

THE DAY AFTER PERFECT

Your Inner Mean-Girl wants you to quit your goal. She tells you that if you can't do it perfectly you might as well not do it at all.

So what are you going to do the day that you mess up? Because making mistakes or missing a day is inevitable. (Remember how you're human?)

Jon Acuff illuminates this in his book "Finish": *"Imperfection is fast, and when it arrives we usually quit. That's why the day-after-perfect is so important. This is the make-or-break day for every goal. This is the day after you skipped the jog. This is the day after you failed to get up early. This is the day after you decided the serving size for a whole box of Krispy Kreme Doughnuts is one. The day after perfect is what separates finishers from starters."*

You wouldn't stop brushing your teeth just because you missed a day or didn't quite reach around your back molars perfectly one night, would you? Of course not!

When you miss a day or mess-up, just pick yourself up and KEEP GOING! Start sloppy and give yourself some grace. That means not punishing yourself by starting back at Day 1; simply carry on from where you left off.

DAY

48

Have you missed a day on this
#1goalfor100days challenge? What are
you going to do when YOU mess-up
or miss a day???

_____

_____

_____

_____

_____

_____

_____

_____

_____

_____

_____

_____

_____

_____

_____

_____

"Missing your goals doesn't make you a failure. It makes you human."

- JOHN C MAXWELL

MARLIESE WILLIAMS BORDMAN: 100 DAYS OF WALKING

After a couple rough years and not taking very good care of myself physically, I decided to make my goal to walk one mile a day for 100 days. I figured I had absolutely nothing to lose. If it didn't work out, any little bit of exercise I got out of it was better than the none I would get without the challenge.

The first couple days felt like a fun new adventure, but it was immediately clear how out of shape I was. I knew I would have to set up some accountability if I wanted to keep it up. I decided to start documenting my journey on social media to hold myself accountable and to possibly motivate friends and clients who might need a little nudge. Before I knew it, I had several friends volunteer to be walking buddies, a built in cheer squad, and people who genuinely wanted to see me succeed.

---

*I have walked a total of **142** miles, lost **13** pounds, and gained a ton of confidence!*

Before long, I was hitting milestones: 10%, 25%, 50% complete! I was increasingly determined to stick with my goal. I walked even when it was inconvenient. Whether that meant walking late in the dark, on busy weekends, getting up early, doing laps around the house, powering through an ice storm, or (my favorite) parking a mile from the stadium and power walking to the Taylor Swift concert! I got to the point that nothing was going to stand in the way of crushing this challenge.

I can't thank Kelli enough for the motivation to get started and what this has done for my self-esteem. This newfound confidence has spilled over into other aspects of my life and has given me the boost I needed to put myself out there both personally and professionally. As I completed Day 100 of the 100-Day Challenge today, I have walked a total of 142 miles, lost 13 pounds, and gained a ton of confidence!

SEASONS OF SACRIFICE

Even though you've fully committed, it's not always going to be easy. Obstacles will arise. Your years-long habit of NOT doing this goal may aggressively tap you on the shoulder and demand the keys back. And it may be tempting to slip back into the comfort of old ways.

Discomfort and sacrifice are necessary if we want to make a lasting change. Think about why this particular goal at this time in your life is worth sacrificing for. What makes it "Worth-It Work" for you?

Whenever you say "YES" to something (i.e. your 100-day goal), you're saying "NO" to something else. As you work through your 100 days, you will be saying "no" to certain things, but not necessarily forever. This is simply one season of your life.

When I committed to writing this book, I sacrificed many things for it. I canceled several things on my calendar, stopped watching as much TV, woke up earlier, and eliminated many of my favorite distractions so that I could focus and get the job done. I knew that it would be a temporary season of sacrifice. It was so hard but so worth it!

What are some sacrifices you're
willing to make for this goal?

"The sacrifice which costs us nothing is worth nothing."

- JEAN JACQUES ROUSSEAU

JESSICA RIEDER: 100 DAYS OF 50 SQUATS

I wanted to prove to myself that I could finish something by doing the 1 Goal for 100 Days challenge! My goal was 50 squats a day.

I loved knowing that so many other people were doing their own goals for 100 days too. Even on days when I struggled, I kept going and pushed through. I didn't let myself come up with excuses. Instead, I worked the challenge into my life.

> *I loved knowing that so many other people were doing their own goals for 100 days too.*

Many days I was able to do 100 squats. I've done squats in 8 different states and even a few times out on my paddle board! It has made me feel more confident in my ability and appearance.

DAY
53

DO THE WORST FIRST

My son trudges downstairs in his pajamas on a Saturday morning. "Why do I have to get dressed and do my chores before I can play video games?" he asks me. Really, it's a rhetorical question. But I answer anyway (in that peppy-mom voice I'm sure he hates): Because in our house, we do the "Worst First."

Doing the Worst First means getting that hard thing out of the way first thing in your day. Brian Tracy, author of *Eat That Frog* says, "The most valuable tasks you can do each day are often the hardest and most complex. But the payoff and rewards for completing these tasks efficiently can be tremendous."

Remember that object lesson where you have a pile of big rocks and a bunch of sand and you have to try to fit them all into a jar? Spoiler: It only works when you put the big rocks (big priorities) in first. Then the sand (everything else on your to-do list) will find a way to fall around them. If you put the sand in first, there won't be enough room for the big rocks.

If you do the hardest (yet often most important things) things FIRST, you'll feel so much more accomplished! Instead of these tasks haunting you for hours, you'll get them out of the way and feel better the rest of the day. And when you feel good, you do good!

"Everyone procrastinates. The difference between high performers and low performers is largely determined by what they choose to procrastinate on." -Brian Tracy

Sometimes the "worst" things—things we are dreading—are actually the BEST things for us! I make it a point to read my scriptures and workout first thing in the morning. Otherwise, it doesn't happen. Putting these things first gives my day a spiritual and physical boost that I never regret.

Do the worst first and I promise, you will build a surge of momentum and accomplishment that will carry you forward!

54

What are the 'big rocks' in your journey, the tasks that are most important for your success? How could you rearrange your daily routine or habits to prioritize these important tasks at the beginning of the day?

"Start by doing what's necessary; then do what's possible; and suddenly you are doing the impossible."

- FRANCIS OF ASSISI

SYDNEY KRESCONKO: 100 DAYS OF INSTAGRAM POSTS

I've now done three rounds of the 1 Goal for 100 Days and kept the goal the same throughout. I really wanted to nail it! I wanted to build a habit of posting daily on my Instagram, which I was doing very inconsistently prior to this. I had the goal of growing my Instagram views and followers so that I could funnel people into my business. I also wanted to simply put out educational and informational niche-related content into the world. So I decided to post everyday on my Instagram, whether a static post or a Reel.

> *This challenge has been a game changer for me, and I plan to use it in the future to build other habits into my daily life.*

After the first round, I noticed that I was trying to rush content and put up simple posts instead of Reels. So I decided to do the challenge again, but this time I marked the difference between when I posted a reel or a regular post. It drastically changed the way I was posting; I post far more reels than anything else now. After completing my third round of the 1 Goal of 100 Days, posting on Instagram has just become a part of my daily routine and a part of my daily business activities. I have come to really enjoy creating content, which came as a surprise. Before, it had been more of a chore. This challenge has been a game changer for me, and I plan to use it in the future to build other habits into my daily life.

THE EASY BUTTON

I was having a bad hair day. It was almost time for my Finally Fearless Podcast interview with Greg McKeown, bestselling author of *Essentialism*. I had learned so much from the book and was excited for the interview. I wanted to look my best—the interview was being video recorded for YouTube and snippets of it would also end up on my Instagram Reels. There was only one problem: my hair was way too greasy and it showed! (Have you ever convinced yourself that you definitely had one more day before you absolutely had to wash your hair, but it turned out that you didn't?)

Normally, I would have complicated the situation by panicking—over-teasing my overly-shiny locks or rushing to the shower and then running out of time. But fresh from reading Greg's book, *Effortless*, (with the very applicable subtitle: Make It Easier to Do What Matters Most), I decided to go with the simplest solution: wear a cute hat. I grabbed a felt fedora and put it on my head. Problem solved!

There have been many times in my life where I've complicated a simple task in an effort to make it better. I mistakenly thought that if it was too easy or simple to accomplish, then it wouldn't be as effective or yield results. I was stuck in the mindset that the hard way was the only way.

Thankfully, Greg's book changed my mind! So did Susie Moore's *Let It Be Easy*. (I'm so lucky to host a podcast that features such brilliant people!) These authors taught me that it was more than okay to embrace ease and the easier path.

I was stuck in the mindset that the hard way was the only way.

When it comes to working towards your goals, take the simplest, easiest path. This will make it easier to be consistent. There's no need to complicate it!

How can you make it "easy"?

"Make everything as easy for yourself as possible. Give yourself every chance. Then you cannot fail."

- ELSIE LINCOLN BENEDICT

ANGELA STEWART: 100 DAYS OF MOVING MY BODY!

I had been meaning to set health and fitness goals since having my last baby right before Covid shut down the world. After she was born, I experienced debilitating back pain that affected my leg and foot. Sometimes I couldn't walk 50 feet without needing to stop and work out terrible muscle cramps. I struggled to even stand for more than 5 minutes to get ready for the day. I finally had back surgery and have been trying to regain strength and mobility since then. Being unable to participate in most activities with my family was not something I was willing to live with. Regaining health and strength after surgery has been essential to participating in all the things with my family!

> *I no longer get to the top of the stairs out of breath.*

Since my surgery, I found that moving my body in any capacity helped with strength and mobility. I decided to focus on daily exercise for my 1 Goal for 100 Days.

I started attending a boot camp (a semi-CrossFit workout) in January and have been continuously attending since then. I have also been walking (sometimes even running!) on a daily basis. I no longer get to the top of the stairs out of breath. My back pain has mostly subsided, and my health is improving! Regaining muscle strength has drastically improved quality of life. Our health is everything!

TRACKING REVEALS TRUTH

My husband and I decided to try and whip our finances into shape. We made a spreadsheet and started tracking where our money went. We were astonished at the percentage of our income that went to eating out! Even taking into account our family size plus inflation and the fact that we live in an expensive city—we were spending A LOT of money at food places. Before this revelation, I would have said we didn't eat out all that much. *But tracking revealed the truth of our spending habits.*

I thought I was eating relatively healthy. Then I started tracking my food on MyFitnessPal, which displays things like sugar content and grams of fat and carbs. Turns out, there's a lot of packaged "health food" that's anything but healthy! *Tracking revealed the truth of my meals.*

My three boys love to race at the go-kart track. My oldest son noticed that after each lap, a screen displays your speed. So he started experimenting with different tactics, tracking his times, and results for each lap. This way, he could see which strategy was most effective and began to improve his overall time, finishing faster in subsequent races. *Tracking revealed the truth of his potential.*

Can you see where I'm going with this? Tracking not only gives you accountability, but revealing information. In our over-scheduled lives, we sometimes experience a bit of brain fog. What we think we're kinda-sorta doing may not be what we're actually doing. By tracking our efforts precisely, we get valuable feedback that exposes areas for improvement.

(Have you downloaded the free 1 Goal for 100 Days Tracker? Scan the QR code at the beginning of this book or get it at www.kellifrance.com/tracker).

What insights has tracking given you so far in this journey? If you haven't started tracking, how might implementing a tracking system improve your consistency or help you identify areas for improvement?

You ever watch an entire Netflix series even when the first episodes are slow, just because someone told you "it gets better"? What if you looked at your goals like that and watched your life get better instead?

MCKENZIE GUYMON: 100 DAYS OF BUSINESS TASKS

When I decided to take the 1 Goal for 100 Days challenge, the timing was terrible. We were packing up and getting ready to move into a new home and everything was in upheaval. But I saw the challenge as a way to keep some kind of routine through all the chaos.

> *Making a point to do the work daily kept me going and absolutely blessed my business.*

My goal for 100 days was to work on daily tasks for my business. While many days this was easy to do, other days were extremely busy and difficult! Making a point to do the work daily kept me going and absolutely blessed my business.

Creating that habit also inspired me to add a few more things to it as I set new goals. I'm grateful for the positive habits I was able to create with my 100 day goal and I can't wait to see what comes from this new one!

INVOLVE YOUR FAMILY

My 9-year-old son was excited about the idea of 1 Goal for 100 Days and asked me to print him the *100-Day Tracker*. He wanted to participate in the very first round! He painstakingly marked off each day as he accomplished his goal and was beaming when he finally crossed the finish line. He was so proud of himself. I was proud of him too. In fact, I saved his tracker as a cherished memory and a reminder that it's never too early to go for your goals!

Just like it's easier for kids to learn another language when their brains are still growing, it's easier to adopt good habits when young. Plus, kids come packaged with that natural energy and enthusiasm. They make great cheerleaders, too! Get your kids, nieces, nephews, husband, sisters, parents, or even your students involved. They might surprise you. They'll definitely inspire you.

How can you involve your family in this?

"The best time to plant a tree was 20 years ago. The second best time is now."

- CHINESE PROVERB

DAY
64

SANDY MUENCH: 100 DAYS OF DEVOTIONS

Devotions are something I do on a regular basis, so I figured it wouldn't be too hard to commit to doing them for 100 days. I had no idea how inconsistent I had been! I also liked the idea of rewarding myself at the end. The most surprising part was that my teenage son joined me on the adventure. He too was drawn in by the idea of a reward. He chose to make his bed. Knowing that we could miss a day and pick right back up gave us both the sense of not failing, just a stumble. So, if we missed a day, we got up the next day and did it again. We both did our task in the morning, so we would check with each other at the breakfast table. I also like how that sparked daily conversation with my son. We finished within five days of the official end date, so we had only missed 5 or fewer mornings in 105 days! Now, I am still doing a daily devotion and he is making his bed every day. Even little goals make a big difference.

LUKE MUENCH (13 YEARS OLD): 100 DAYS OF MAKING MY BED

My mom was doing this 100 day thing for a purse, so I thought it would be a good way to get a Lego set. I decided to make my bed because I don't make my bed, and my mom and dad are always bugging me about it. It wasn't hard at all. It wasn't even a pain in the butt to do it. I got up, got dressed and made my bed. It took me less than a minute. If I didn't get it made in the morning, I made sure I made my bed before I went to bed. If I didn't make it at least an hour before bed, it didn't count. I still make my bed every day, not with the same neat effort that I used during the challenge, but it's made. I don't even think much about it.

> *Doing the same thing for that long makes it a habit and now its just something I do.*

EVERYTHING TO LOSE

I once read an article about a mom who was trying to motivate her child to clean his room. Bribery was ineffective. Reward charts were NOT working. So she decided to take a different approach. This mom took a clear glass jar and filled it with thirty one-dollar bills. At the beginning of the month, she set the jar in her child's room and told him that the money was his; he could spend it at the end of the month. However, there was a catch. For every day she saw his room was dirty, she would take a dollar out of the jar.

The first day she found clothes on the floor and took a dollar bill out of the jar. Her son was devastated. Now he only had twenty-nine dollars!

The next day she discovered his toys on the floor and took a dollar out of the jar. Her son started to catch on. If he wanted to have lots of money by the end of the month, he needed to keep his room clean! The third day it was clean. The fourth day it was clean. Soon keeping his room clean became a habit, which made it easier to keep up. By the end of the month, the son had kept twenty seven dollars. This was a win-win situation for both of them.

In a 2016 study scientists from the University of Pennsylvania asked people to walk 7,000 steps a day for six months. Some participants were paid $1.40 for each day they achieved their goal, while others lost $1.40 if they failed to. The second group hit their daily target 50% more often.

I was inspired to use this approach on myself when my sister and I participated in a goal challenge together. Growing up, we'd always stolen each other's favorite clothes to wear. But now that she lived hundreds of miles away, raiding her closet wasn't so easy. We each owned a skirt the other loved and envied. So we came up with a motivational deal to connect to our goal: whoever missed a day of the challenge would have to give their cherished skirt to the other. I didn't want to lose my skirt! It was a powerful motivator for me. (More powerful than it was for my sister, apparently, who ended up having to mail me her skirt! I wear it when she visits. Because that's what sisters are for.)

Sometimes an incentive reward works (making a chart, or promising yourself a reward at the end of a difficult task) and sometimes it helps to already have what you want in your hands and do whatever it takes not to lose it.

Write down five things you already own and cherish. Can you think of a way to use them as a unique incentive to encourage your progress?

"It's not hard to make decisions when you know what your values are."

- ROY DISNEY

DAY

67

MARY F. MURPHY: 100 DAYS OF EXERCISE

I have maintained a pretty good level of fitness my whole life, but now that I'm over 50, I felt the need to be active every single day. Motion is lotion! And I want to age well.

For this challenge I decided to be active and exercise for 100 days in a row! This meant finding time to exercise on cold days, hot days, travel days (I walked 2 miles in the airport once, waiting for flight), and regular busy days—not letting excuses derail me!

Every day in January I walked or ran at least 1 mile (usually 2+) OUTSIDE in the Boston area. I hate the cold. But I did it anyway!

> *This meant not letting excuses derail me!*

In February, I exercised for at least 28 min every day— running, walking, Peloton, or fitness class.

In March, I set a goal to get in 100 miles of run or walk and repeated this strategy in April. Between menopause and other challenges that come with aging, being active every day isn't a nicety—it's a necessity!

IF IT WAS FUN, IT WOULD ALREADY BE DONE

Is it weird that I sometimes get excited to get on the treadmill? It's not because I like to exercise (I don't!), but because I like to watch my favorite show (Virgin River, anyone?). Lately I've combined the two to make my treadmill time a lot more fun. Whe we were all kids, we instinctively knew how to have fun. It came naturally. We didn't have the "shoulds" of society echoing in our ears. We didn't have as many emotional scars. Ignorance was bliss. We were simply free and we felt more alive.

Fast-forward to adulthood. We have so many more responsibilities than we did as kids. We often get stuck in survival mode. We have hundreds of hurts. And frankly, we're tired so it can seem a lot harder to find opportunities to have fun.

But I believe there's always a way to make things more fun:

1. Add a Competitive Element: Who doesn't love a chance to win? Make a bet or set a prize with your Accountability Partner to raise the stakes!

2. Add Music: Music has the power to affect our mood. Create a special playlist to set the right atmosphere for your goal.

3. Create a Positive Environment: The Danish have a word for this is *hygge*. It means "a quality of coziness and comfort." Setting has a huge impact on our experience. Make sure the environment is comfortable, well-lit, and aesthetically pleasing.

My Mom once told me, "If it was fun, it would already be done." When you make your goal more fun, it makes it so much easier to get the job done.

How can you incorporate more fun or
enjoyment into the process to make
your goal more exciting?

JESSICA STEWART: 100 DAYS OF READING THE BIBLE

I have wanted to read the Bible in its entirety for several years and actually even tried a few times, but it was hard. I'd start, then lose ambition. Then, just before the New Year, I saw Kelli's social media post about her 100 Day Challenge. Immediately below Kelli's post was a friend's video talking about how she read the Bible that year and was planning on doing it again. Her post spoke to me and I was like, "Okay God, I see you taking my excuses away AND giving me an accountability plan." It was my year to make this happen!

I didn't have time to sit down and read the Bible like I wanted to. I run two small businesses, work a full-time day-job, have a husband, adult kids, grandkids, and pets! Additionally, I found my mind wandering as I read. That's when thinking outside the box came into play! I have a 45 min drive home each day, so I decided to download the free Holy Bible app (side note: I really like that I could customize the voice, highlight verses, read along when time or circumstances allowed, and even speed it up if I wanted to). In between the client calls I normally make on my commute, I felt like I could carve out at least 15-20 mins of the travel time to listen to the verses. This system took away my excuses: *I'm busy, I'm sick, I'm tired, my eyes hurt, gripe, gripe, gripe.* If the car ride wasn't an option, then I'd listen while I was taking a shower, getting ready for work, feeding animals, or making lunch.

> *It took me 107 days to complete the 100 day challenge and I won't apologize for being human and falling behind.*

Find what works for you and eliminate the excuses before they start. You know yourself best so be proactive while you're fired up with excitement to achieve your goal to help you stay motivated. Don't be afraid to take an untraditional approach to accomplishing your goal. I found myself craving my "me time". I travel frequently and I got sick for 2 weeks. I missed days. But instead of throwing in the towel, I opened the app and listened. It took me 107 days to complete the 100 day challenge and I won't apologize for being human and falling behind. The fact that I did something that I'd been saying I was gonna do for years, made me pretty dang proud of myself!!!

DAY

70

YOU ARE NOT TOO OLD & IT IS NOT TOO LATE

Don't listen to your Inner Critic who loves to tell you that it's too late or you're too old. There is still time to be who you want to be.

- Stan Lee created "Fantastic Four" at age 39.

- Fashion designer Vera Wang designed her first dress at 40.

- Sam Walton founded the first Walmart at age 44.

- Henry Ford was 45 when he created the revolutionary Model T car in 1908.

- Julia Child published her first cookbook at 50.

- Betty White didn't become an icon until she joined the cast of "The Mary Tyler Moore Show" in 1973 at age 51.

- Arianna Huffington started her namesake publication when she was 55-years-old.

- Colonel Sanders was 62 when he franchised Kentucky Fried Chicken

- Laura Ingalls Wilder published the first of the "Little House" books at age 65.

- Writer Harry Bernstein authored countless rejected books before getting his first hit at age 96.

- Jack Weil was 45 when he founded what became the most popular cowboy-wear brand, Rockmount Ranch Wear. He remained its CEO until he died at the ripe old age of 107 in 2008.

- And finally, MY MOM went to a Weezer concert when she was 70.

It is never too late to live the life you want!

What are some things you've told
yourself are out of your reach because
of your age? How can you rewrite
that story?

"The best way to gain self-confidence is to do what you are afraid to do."

- SWATI SHARMA

KARI STANDFUSS: 100 DAYS OF SWAPPING SODA FOR 100 OZ OF WATER

I knew that I needed to increase my water intake and cut out the excess empty calories with the soda I drank all the time. I have been wanting to lose some weight and the empty calories were not helping me. So I chose to cut myself off from soda and drink 100 ounces of water every day instead! This goal was not easy because every Friday and Saturday night my family has movie night—complete with soda and popcorn!

> *I was so happy I participated in the challenge and I have continued the goal since I started.*

This goal helped jumpstart my weight loss journey because in the 100 days I lost 15 pounds. I also noticed a difference in my skin and nails not being so dry. I was so happy I participated in the challenge and I have continued the goal since I started.

YOU CAN DO BIG BRAVE THINGS

You don't need to have a fancy degree.

You don't need to have the entire plan laid out.

You don't need to have all your ducks in a row.

You don't need to know ALL the things.

You don't need to have several years of experience.

You can do BIG brave things!

You simply need to

Start Small,

Start Slow,

Start Sloppy.

Write out all the excuses you've used to hold yourself back. Then cross them out and reframe them. What Big Brave things are you longing to accomplish?

You can Do Big, Brave things.

THE HARD IS WHAT MAKES IT GREAT

I recently watched an old favorite movie, "A League of Our Own". In this film, Dottie, played by Geena Davis, gets discouraged and decides to quit playing baseball.

"It just got too hard," she says to Coach Jimmy, when he asks why she's resigning.

Tom Hanks, who plays Coach Jimmy, tells it to her like it is: "It's supposed to be hard. If it wasn't hard, everyone would do it. **The hard is what makes it great.**"

Have you ever felt like Dottie? Ever been so discouraged when things seemed hard that you wanted to quit?

This was me when we bought our second Airbnb. We had only seen this house once via Zoom because it was in a different state than us. We had no idea what we were really getting into.

I remember walking into it for the very first time. When I looked around at the hot mess of a house **I thought to myself, "Have we just made the biggest mistake of our lives with this purchase?"** I was overwhelmed with the difficult work that laid ahead of us. It was going to be so hard to somehow make this outdated 80's home look gorgeous. But we got to work and it paid off! The house turned out amazing and so unique. In the words of Tom Hanks, it was the hard that made it great!

Going for goals is tough but, Girl, so are you

When we get in the driver's seat of our goal-getter journey, we often start out all starry-eyed with a romanticized view of what going for our goals will look like. We are ignorant to the fact that it will be hard. We don't take into account that we will run into roadblocks, traffic jams, and speed bumps. These are a very normal part of the journey. Then when we get stuck in traffic, we complain, as if we are surprised. But this is what we signed up for when we put our hands on the steering wheel. It's all part of the process of driving towards your goal. We might get muddy or have to take a detour along the way but we will get there if we are patient and persevere.

When you get overwhelmed or discouraged, don't worry, that's a normal part of it. Keep going. You'll figure it out as you go. Everything worthwhile is hard before it is easy.

Going for goals is tough but, girl, so are you.

Have you come across difficulties in the 1 Goal for 100 Days yet? How did you push through and continue despite the challenges? If they haven't come up yet, how WILL you push through and continue with your goal?

"The difference between winning and losing is most often not quitting."

- WALT DISNEY

MOTIVATION IS A MYTH

I literally had no motivation to write this page. If I would have waited for the motivation to write it, you wouldn't be reading this page right now—ha!

Most of us believe we need to wait for motivation to hit us in order to get anything done. We want it to strike us like a lightning bolt that a sudden boost of energy and passion. We are like a new toy at Christmas, just waiting for the battery. But the battery is not included.

Spoiler alert: Motivation is a myth.

Most people get stuck in the Motivation Trap. This myth can be a trap that keeps us stuck. If you wait around for motivation, you might be waiting for a long time. No amount of inspirational cat posters, cutesy quotes, or caffeine will do the trick when it comes to motivation.

How, then, do we keep persevering when we don't feel like it? Because let's be honest, there will be many moments when we don't feel like it.

In the words of my Podcaster friend, Angie Lee, "Ready is a Lie." We will never be ready, so we must start before we are ready. You won't always be motivated so you must learn to be disciplined.

Rubin Khoddam, a Clinical Psychologist in L.A. explains, "Motivation does not precede action. Action precedes motivation. I don't just mean any action. I mean committed action. Valued action. What is valued action? Valued actions are actions that are consistent with your values in life. These are actions that are consistent with the type of person you want to be. I value staying healthy, so I set a goal for myself to go to exercise at least four days a week. My valued action is getting my butt up and going to the gym regardless of whether I am in the mood or not."

Instead of waiting around for motivation, take disciplined action that aligns with your values.

What are your Core Values? Are your
goals aligned with them to help you
overcome the Motivation Trap?

BECOMING

When I look at my goals with the mindset of becoming, it helps me focus on my Why more. It makes the goal become part of my identity and who I am. It lets me look at my goals in a different light. Instead of focusing on what NOT to do (DON'T sleep in! DON'T go over budget! DON'T order fries!), I focus on the process of BECOMING a specific characteristic. When I put my goals in the perspective of PROCESS, rather than RESULT, it drastically shifts my mindset.

Right now, my focus is on becoming healthy. Trying to BECOME healthy looks very different than just avoiding junk food. It means I act like a healthy person—that I eat more fruits and veggies, drink more water, take the stairs, and have treats only occasionally.

It means utilizing my standing desk more, making more home-cooked meals, and taking my dog on daily walks. BECOMING healthy means being an example of health and fitness for my family.

So I've recommitted to eating veggies at every meal and moving my body everyday for 30 minutes at least 5 days a week. And on days where I don't feel like doing it, I remind myself this: I am the type of person who moves her body everyday. That affirmation always seems to help! Try it today: **I am the type of person who** _____

Becoming is a journey and that journey takes time. I know I will make mistakes but I'll continue to try until it becomes a part of my identity.

Have you been focusing on the end result or the process of BECOMING a specific characteristic? How does viewing your goal as a process rather than a result impact your mindset and approach to it?

"*I didn't really know what I wanted to do, but I knew the woman I wanted to become.*"

— DIANE VON FURSTENBERG

TAMARA BABULSKI: 100 DAYS OF JOURNALING

I had always struggled with self-confidence. That is, until I took up Kelli's challenge and started journaling. At first, I journaled to tell off my Inner Mean Girl. I spent the entire pages of one journal telling my Inner Mean Girl (I call her Melissa) to stop berating me and wrote about how I wasn't going to listen to her anymore. Then I got a new journal. This one was focused on finding the "new" me.

> *Thanks to the 1 Goal for 100 Days challenge, I am not going back to being a wallflower.*

Through journaling, I re-branded myself as a pixie. Pixies are mischievous and daring, bold yet childlike. This is the new me. Journaling helped me document my adventures as a pixie: I dyed my hair green and went around a huge conference finding everyone with green hair. I was able to make 23 new friends—just by finding common hair color! Thanks to the 1 Goal for 100 Days challenge, I am not going back to being a wallflower; rather, this pixie is enlarging her circle and gaining confidence with every stroke of the pen.

YOUR LONGING IS YOUR CALLING

Have you ever scrolled social media and been stung by feelings of jealousy? Maybe you see someone has incredible taste or a remarkable talent or an amazing partner or a successful business or gets to travel the world. But jealousy can work to your advantage. It's your unconscious mind tapping you on the shoulder and whispering, "Pssst, we want that, too."

As you contemplate your goals this year, consider **what you have been longing for.**

What are you excited or curious about?

What do you get jealous about?

What do you wish would happen?

What would you do or become if you knew you couldn't fail?

Those sparks of excitement aren't just random. And they aren't universal—not everyone has your unique combination of interests. These sparks are talking to YOU. They are your calling.

Don't ignore them or let your Inner Mean-Girl talk you out of those longings. They are connected to your purpose! Go after them!

In the wise words of author Elizabeth Gilbert: "If you've lost your life's true passion (or if you're struggling desperately to find passion in the first place), don't sweat it. Back off for a while. But don't go idle, either. Just try something different, something you don't care about so much. Why not try following mere curiosity, with its humble, roundabout magic? At the very least, it will keep you pleasantly distracted while life sorts itself out. At the very most, your curiosity may surprise you. Before you even realize what's happening, it may have led you safely all the way home."

Think of a time when jealousy made you yearn for something someone else had or achieved. What was it that sparked your jealousy, and what did you wish for in that moment? How does that point you toward your true desires and passions?

Things that excite you are not random. They are connected to your purpose. Follow them.

HOW DO YOU WANT TO FEEL?

On a call with my business coach, I shared my goals with her:

"Those sound great," she said, taking my ambition in stride. "But how do you want to FEEL?"

Her question stopped me in my tracks. I had always made goals just to make goals; I hadn't ever thought about them through the lens of emotion.

I instantly thought, "JOY!" I want to feel more joy & less stress.

Since then, I've been centering goals around those feelings and I love the direction it's given me. Focusing on the FEELINGS I want to have has been much more intentional and effective. It made me realize WHY I should (or shouldn't!) engage in certain tasks and goals...because I want to feel more joy.

I dare you to try it.

What emotions do YOU want to feel as
you work toward your goal?

"Your level of success will rarely exceed your level of personal development because success is something you attract by the person you become."

- JIM ROHN

PIGGYBACK YOUR HABITS

You already have hundreds of habits you've created over the course of your life. Whether good (waking up early, brushing your teeth, hugging your kids) or bad (staying up too late, eating out every meal, checking your Instagram 20 times a day), our consistent behaviors become second nature to our lives. As you try to adopt a new habit during these 100 days, it might help to pair it with one you already have down! For example:

- *After I brush my teeth, I'll do my 10 squats.*

- *Every time I pick up my phone to check social media, I'll go to the Notes app first and write down one thing I'm grateful for.*

- *After I change into my pajamas, I'll sit in the closet and meditate for 15 minutes.*

When I began building my business, I made a goal to post on social media three times a day to gain momentum. But it was hard! I wasn't used to posting that much. Then, I had the thought: *"I eat three times a day—I never forget to do that! So why don't I use mealtimes as a trigger? Every time I eat, I'll post on social media."* The pairing up of a new habit with an old one worked like a charm.

What are some of the habits you have down so that you never have to think about them? Which of these might pair well with your new 100 Day Habit and why?

DAY

86

"*I would rather be a hot mess of bold action, a make-it-happen-learn-on-the-fly kind of person, than a perfectly organized coward.*"

- BRENDON BURCHARD

IT'S OKAY TO BE A COPYCAT WHEN IT COMES TO GOALS

When I was a freshman in high school, a girl named Tracy moved into my neighborhood. She came from California and had a fun and spunky personality. Her hair color changed with every season (she grew up to become a hairstylist) and she was artistically talented, especially with photography. We loved hanging out together!

We used to dress up in fashionable clothes and take photos of each other with her big film camera. These photoshoots would take place at her house or in a nearby abandoned barn. This sparked a love for photography in me. My artistic self felt awakened! However, I remember thinking that photography was Tracy's hobby and that I shouldn't copy her. So I didn't.

This teenage logic was completely faulty. But my negative self-talk stopped me from investing more time or serious interest in that hobby as a young person.

Years later, as a new mom, I took a film photography class and my love for the camera was rekindled. I moved into an online class and began shooting images of my friends and family for practice.

I went on to become a professional portrait photographer for 13 years. I taught other photographers how to improve their skills and run successful businesses. My husband and I even started an online photography school and magazine called Chic Critique, and hosted multiple retreats for photographers.

I had a truly full-circle moment when I got to photograph Tracy's family in a portrait session.

Don't let that negative voice in your head tell you that you can't do something simply because someone else does it.

Is there something you've held back
from exploring or doing because you
were worried you'd be "copying?"

DAY

88

" *Waiting for perfect is never as smart as making progress.* "

- SETH GODIN

BELIEVE TO ACHIEVE

One of the keys to sticking with your goals is believing that you can achieve them. If you believe you can, you're halfway there. Doubts will arise. Your Inner Mean Girl will try to stop you. Life will get in the way. But if you believe you can do this, you will. Henry Ford once said, "Whether you think you can, or you think you can't—you're right."

Belief is the best weapon that will help you fight off your Inner Mean Girl and win. It will help you stay the course regardless of what comes your way. You don't need to have confidence in your ability to do something, you just need confidence in your ability to figure it out. Psychologist Maud Purcell, explains, "True confidence develops from an increasing belief that you can rely on yourself to take action and follow through, no matter what the result." Stay strong in your belief. Doubt your doubts.

> *"Whether you think you can, or you think you can't—you're right." -Henry Ford*

BORROW BELIEF

If you struggle with your belief in yourself or your ability to do this, just remember that I BELIEVE IN YOU. This might sound cliché or corny but it's true. One of the gifts God has blessed me with is seeing monumental potential in other people, even when they don't see it themselves. I can visualize what others can become beyond what most can visualize for themselves and their future. I see people for what they could become instead of who they are now.

And sometimes just knowing that someone out there has faith in us is all we need to move forward to the next level. Belief is everything.

But sometimes you have to BORROW BELIEF and if that's the case, you can always always borrow mine. I'm here for you, girl!

Take on the point of view of someone who absolutely believes in your capability and potential (ie ME!) and write yourself a letter of encouragement from her point of view.

YOU CAN'T AMAZON-PRIME YOUR RESULTS

In this world of instant messaging, on-demand movies, and 2-day shipping, it's easy to also expect instant results with our goals. Unfortunately, it's not a crossover concept.

I've been an entrepreneur for over 20 years and the one thing I've learned is that it takes TIME (lots and lots of time) to make progress and get results! It's all about daily consistent effort.

My husband and I have moved our family a lot and every time I started a new photography business in a new area it took me about 2 YEARS to gain momentum and get a clientele.

I've seen many entrepreneurs start a new business venture and then say it's not for them because they were not making big bucks 3 months in. That's simply not realistic! Very few small businesses make much profit their first year—if they make any profit at all.

The same rule of thumb can be applied to most new ventures, including our fitness goals. My friend, who lost almost 100 lbs a few years ago, gave me the best advice: *Give yourself a solid year of consistent effort when you're trying to transform your body.*

Changing and Becoming take time, so be patient with the process and focus on the behaviors and not so much the results. That seed you planted will eventually bloom!

Have you ever experienced impatience with a goal or a desire for instant gratification? What behaviors or habits are you willing to focus on for the long-term benefit?

"The day you plant the seed is not the day you eat the fruit. Be patient and stay the course."

- FABIENNE FREDRICKSON

ONE DAY AT A TIME, ONE MINUTE AT A TIME

There were several days on my own 100-day journey where I got overwhelmed by how far I had to go. It's easy to get overwhelmed by the big picture. The idea of doing something for 100 days can feel like a lot. When you feel yourself getting overwhelmed, zoom in. The solution is to break it down into bite-size pieces, focusing on one day at a time. You can do anything for one day!

When I got overwhelmed, I had to remind myself that I only have to do it for one day, consistently. This mindset hack helped me make it through the daunting days when I felt inundated with stress and doubt. Like my mom used to say, "You eat an elephant one bite at a time." (Personally, the idea of eating an elephant makes me dry-heave, but you get the point).

Another hack I use is to tell myself that I only have to do it for one minute. Sometimes the hardest part is getting started. Telling myself that I only have to do something for sixty seconds motivates me juuuuust enough to start. And once I start, I begin to feel the momentum that makes me want to continue doing it for longer than one minute.

"You will never win if you never begin." -Helen Rowland

Take this journey one day at a time, or even one minute at a time. You can do anything for one day or one minute!

How can showing up for even one minute on the hard days help you reach your ultimate goal?

"If you aim at nothing, you'll hit it every time."

- ZIG ZIGLAR

DONE IS BETTER THAN PERFECT

I've done several rounds of 1 Goal for 100 Days (it's addicting!) but I have a confession: I haven't always made it through. During one of the challenges, I got caught in the dreaded perfection trap. I did my goal for about 50 days and then I missed a day. Then I missed another day. And another. I had procrastinated printing out my 100-day tracker (found at kellifrance.com/tracker) so I wasn't even sure what day I was on. Unfortunately, that was enough to make me quit entirely on my goal.

Looking back, I realized that my perfectionism was the main reason I gave up. My subconscious thought was that if I couldn't do it perfectly, I might as well not do it at all.

When perfectionists realize that we can't do something perfectly, we see it almost as permission to stop because we can't possibly make changes without perfection. This is a huge lie!

Therapists call this cognitive distortion "All or Nothing Thinking". Other names for these lies are "Black and White Thinking" or "Polarized Thinking".

Perfectionism= Fear

Perfectionism is just fear in disguise. Perfectionists often have the fear that any imperfection or failure will result in rejection, humiliation, disappointment, or judgment from others. So we strive for perfection as a way to prevent or minimize these anxieties. Perfectionism is just a fear of failure which stops us from completing our work and, even worse, stops us from beginning our work. When we feel pressure to perform perfectly it makes tasks feel monumental and overwhelming. Because we think we have to do them flawlessly, we get overwhelmed at the idea of starting or continuing. In the words of Catherine Carrigan, **"Perfect is the enemy of done."**

Perfectionism is a distraction. Author Jon Acuff explains how we use fear as a Survival Strategy to distract us from our fear of rejection. "Perfectionism offers us two distinct distractions: Hiding places and Noble obstacles. A hiding place is an activity you focus on instead of your goal. A noble obstacle is a virtuous-sounding reason for not working toward a finish. Both are toxic to your ability to finish."

What we don't realize is that we can make change and impact others even when we perform at levels that are "good enough." My mom keeps a quote in her house that says, "Use what talent you possess: the woods would be very silent if no birds sang except those that sang best."

> *"Use what talent you possess: the woods would be very silent if no birds sang except those that sang best."*

The solution to this All OR Nothing thinking is to use the word AND instead. Change your mindset from "I can do my goal perfectly some days OR not at all" to "I can do my goal perfectly some days AND imperfectly on other days." Go from polarizing thoughts like, "I can have only good days OR give up entirely when I have a bad day" to "I can have good days AND bad days".

95

How can you break out of perfectionist thinking? How can you use the word AND instead of OR when you catch yourself in All or Nothing Thinking?

"I cannot even tell you how many plans I have "violently executed" by the seat of my pants, rather than waiting for things to be perfect. In fact, I have written every single one of my books that way — in stolen moments, as efficiently as I can, and constantly letting things slide that are not ideal. Remember that 80% is better than 100% and done is better than perfect."

- ELIZABETH GILBERT

DAY
96

BURN THE BOATS

In the early 1500s, a Spanish explorer named Cortez arrived in the "New World" with the intention to conquer the continent. But his men were tired from the long and disease-ridden journey across the ocean. They were in a strange new place and the native people weren't friendly. (Probably because the Aztecs guessed what Cortez wanted—gold and power at any price.) In any case, Cortez's men weren't feeling the same conquering enthusiasm as he was. So Cortez ordered all their ships to be burned. It sent a clear message to the men: *We win or we die, but there's no going back.*

While it's obviously not admirable to crush out a civilization for wealth and power, we can still learn from the fiery object lesson. When we remove our escape hatch, and the only way out becomes through, our dedication to the problem at hand gets our attention in a whole new way.

I know a woman who was tired of her corporate job and wanted to start her own business. She did both for a while, but eventually, she realized she'd need a lot more time for her new venture if it was going to succeed. So she quit her job. She gave up a comfy salary and health benefits. If she was going to survive, her business would have to make it. She burned her boats and scared herself into the success she truly wanted.

During this 1 Goal for 100 Days Challenge, you are in the middle of undergoing a major transformation, of forging new neural pathways, and habits. It's important to cut off your old way of doing things. Burn the boats. Failure is not an option.

Can you identify any aspects of your life or goals where you might need to adopt a "burn the boats" mentality to achieve success?

THERE'S NO SUCH THING AS COASTING

Imagine riding your bike up a steep hill. You stand as you pedal, sweat trickling from beneath your helmet, quads burning. Finally, you crest the top of the hill and rest your legs a moment, letting the momentum carry you down the other side. You've earned a bit of coasting!

Haven't you?

You let gravity carry you. You close your eyes, appreciating the breeze on your sweaty face and the feeling of accomplishment. Suddenly, the breeze dies out. You open your eyes. You've stopped! What happened?

With goals, there's no such thing as coasting. You're either moving forward or moving backward. If we're not progressing, then we are sliding back.

I experienced this first-hand when our family moved to California just before the holidays. It was a big adjustment during a hectic and busy time. Before the move, I'd been really consistent with my fitness goals and thought I'd be okay taking a break. But once I got back into my routines after the move, I felt the difference! I noticed I wasn't as strong as I used to be. Some of the workout moves I had considered easy felt HARD. I hadn't been coasting. I was moving backward!

Rather than beating myself up about it or fixating on all my (very legitimate) excuses, I decided to start again. There was no denying that I'd gone backward, but at least now I was moving in the right direction.

What steps can you take to regain momentum and get back on track with your goals, even if you've experienced a setback or taken a break? How will you ensure you're always moving forward in your journey?

A GOAL IS A PROMISE YOU MAKE TO YOURSELF

A goal is a commitment. When you give up or quit, you've broken the promise you made to yourself. If you break enough of these promises, you start to doubt yourself. If you quit on yourself enough times, it becomes your identity.

When you don't keep your promises to yourself, you won't believe in your ability to do the next goal. This is why I want you to succeed! I want you to identify yourself as someone who shows up for herself, instead of someone who gives up on herself. I want you to finish your 100 Days so that you can learn to trust yourself again.

Trust is a major component to any good relationship, including the one with yourself. Trust is earned by consistently being there for someone, including yourself. Trust comes from honoring your commitments to yourself and keeping promises (aka goals) to yourself.

Think about it: The best relationships you have are often with people who continue to show up for you. They are there for you on good and bad days, in sickness and in health. In order to have a good relationship with yourself, you need to do the same by showing up for yourself consistently.

When you keep your promises to yourself, it makes it easier to keep the next promise (goal). So show up for yourself every day for the next 100 days and I promise, you will have a better relationship with yourself and feel more confident because you are keeping your word to yourself.

Have you ever broken a promise to yourself? How did it impact your self-trust? Think about your current 100-Day Goal. How can you use this opportunity to build trust and confidence in yourself?

DAY 100: YOU DID IT!

You did it! You freakin' did it!!! Doing 100 days of anything is a HUGE DEAL!

I am SO incredibly proud of you! I hope you are so proud of yourself! Don't for one second discredit or downplay this accomplishment. It took a ton of commitment and consistency. Be sure to take some time to pause and celebrate this amazing achievement.

I hope you feel more confident now. William Jennings Bryan says that "The way to develop self-confidence is to do the thing you fear and get a record of successful experiences behind you." You now have a record of 100 successful experiences behind you! That's a LOT of wins to be proud of!

NOW SHARE IT

Inspire others to start their 100 day journey by sharing that you accomplished yours. Be sure to use the hashtag #1Goalfor100Days and tag me at @kellifrance so I can celebrate with you too!

P.S. I'd love to hear how this 1 Goal for 100 Days has helped you. Please share your story with me at kelli@kellifrance.com or via DM at instagram.com/kellifrance.

100

WRITE YOURSELF A LETTER OF
CONGRATULATIONS and reflect on
how these last 100 days changed you.

ABOUT THE AUTHOR

Meet **Kelli France**, Confidence Queen. Kelli is your girl-next-door bestie with a zest for life. Her journey from **food-stamps to seven-figures** is not just a testament to her grit, but a story she shares to inspire others. As a Confidence Coach, Kelli helps women get out of their own way and go for their goals.

Kelli wears many hats, including that of the beloved host of the Finally Fearless Podcast. With its extraordinary impact, it has earned a well-deserved place among the top 1% of podcasts worldwide.

Kelli is not just about words; she's about action. She hosts a virtual sisterhood of over 5,000 women in her confidence-boosting book club, diving into the pages of personal growth and ending with insights straight from the authors themselves.

Family is the core of Kelli's world. She is the mom of 4 hilarious kids whose personalities are like salsa; hot, medium, mild, and pico. She and her husband of 23 years have shared a tradition of weekly date nights since they were newlyweds.

Residing near sunny San Diego, Kelli enjoys the simple pleasures of life: one taco, one beach day, and one Bachelor episode at a time.

Kelli is all about embracing confidence, courage, and the perfect slice of pizza—and she's here to make sure you savor every slice of your life too. Join the confidence movement at @kellifrance on Instagram for your daily dose of fun, inspiration, and confidence boosts.

Made in USA - Kendallville, IN
50775_9798871681169
12.28.2023 1327